Five Public Philosophies of
WALTER LIPPMANN

5 PUBLIC PHILOSOPHIES OF Walter Lippmann

by Benjamin F. Wright

UNIVERSITY OF TEXAS PRESS AUSTIN

Grateful acknowledgment is given to the following publishers for their permission to reprint selections from Walter Lippmann's books:

The Macmillan Company for *Public Opinion* (Copyright 1922 and renewed 1950 by Walter Lippmann), *The Phantom Public* (Copyright 1925 and renewed 1953 by Walter Lippmann), *A Preface to Morals* (Copyright 1929 and renewed 1957 by Walter Lippmann), *The Method of Freedom* (Copyright 1934 and renewed 1962 by Walter Lippmann), and *The New Imperative* (Copyright 1935 and renewed 1963 by Walter Lippmann).

George Allen and Unwin Ltd. for *Public Opinion* (Copyright 1922 and renewed 1950 by Walter Lippmann).

Atlantic–Little, Brown and Co. for *The Good Society* (Copyright 1936, 1937, 1943, © renewed 1971 by Walter Lippmann) and *The Public Philosophy* (Copyright 1955 by Walter Lippmann).

First paperback printing, 2015

Library of Congress Cataloging in Publication Data

Wright, Benjamin Fletcher, 1900–
Five public philosophies of Walter Lippmann.

Bibliography: p.
1. Lippmann, Walter, 1889–   I. Title.
JC251.L55W7   320.5'092'4   73-6696
ISBN 978-1-4773-0529-4

To Peter and David

CONTENTS

Introduction 9

1. The Age of Youthful Optimism 17
   A Preface to Politics (1913) p. 17
   Drift and Mastery (1914) p. 26

2. Democracy and the Defects of Public Opinion . . 38
   Public Opinion (1922) p. 38
   The Phantom Public (1925) p. 58

3. The State as Mediator 65
   A Preface to Morals (1929) p. 65

4. Security through a Compensated Economy . . 71
   The Method of Freedom (1934) p. 71
   The New Imperative (1935) p. 83

5. The Free Market, Civility, and Natural Law . . 87
   The Good Society (1937) p. 87
   Essays in the Public Philosophy (1955) p. 115

6. From Scientific Realism to Romantic Renaissance . 133

Bibliography 159

Index 163

INTRODUCTION

In their recent anthology, *The Essential Lippmann*, Professors Clinton Rossiter and James Lare begin with this assessment: "This treasury of the writings of Walter Lippmann is a witness to our conviction that he is perhaps the most important political thinker of the twentieth century."[1] In an essay in the volume presented to Mr. Lippmann on his seventieth birthday, James Reston, who, with Marquis Childs, edited the book, remarks that "no doubt Walter Lippmann, at seventy, would prefer to be judged by his books of political philosophy."[2]

Whether Lippmann would "prefer to be judged by his books of political philosophy," I do not know. Whether he is the "most important political thinker" of this century is at least questionable. He is, in my opinion, the most versatile, the most wide ranging, and in some respects the most impressive. Certainly he has varied more widely in his views than any other significant political theo-

[1] Clinton Rossiter and James Lare (eds.), *The Essential Lippmann*, p. xi.
[2] Marquis Childs and James Reston (eds.), *Walter Lippmann and His Times*, p. 229. The book contains essays by an impressive group: Childs, Carl Binger, George F. Kennan, Allan Nevins, Arthur Krock, Raymond Aron, Iverach McDonald, Frank Moraes, Harry S. Ashmore, Reinhold Niebuhr, Arthur Schlesinger, Jr., and Reston. Only Arthur Schlesinger deals primarily with Lippmann as political philosopher. The others are concerned with Lippmann as journalist or as commentator on foreign affairs.

rist of his time. Between 1913 and 1955 he wrote an immense amount on foreign policy, as well as his editorials, essays, and, especially, his syndicated column, "Today and Tomorrow." The writings on foreign affairs, in books or essays or columns, will not be discussed. That is a large subject and deserves separate treatment. Nor will his various brief writings on domestic affairs be considered. It is not that they are irrelevant, but rather that my intent is to consider one aspect of his writings—what James Reston refers to as his books of political philosophy.

That Mr. Lippmann has been one of the two or three leading journalists of the century is a proposition with which few would disagree. He has carried on the personal journalism of such editors as Horace Greeley, Henry Watterson, and William Allen White, and, on the whole, has done it superbly.[3] That extraordinary career has been the subject of discussion by others, though no one has done much more than offer relatively brief comments on the range of Lippmann's journalistic writings. But in this study, to repeat, there will be no attempt to remedy that defect. No other person of his time and country has so persistently and from so many points of view analyzed some of the basic issues of political philosophy in a series of books that avoided both the pedantic and the merely contemporary and that have received even less overall consideration than his discussions of foreign policy or his editorials, essays, and columns.

In *The Essential Lippmann* Professors Rossiter and Lare, who do not limit their selections to his books, organize his writings over more than half a century under eleven headings.[4] This systematic classification has no clear relation to any of Lippmann's

[3] See David Elliott Weingast, *Walter Lippmann: A Study in Personal Journalism*, as well as most of the essays in the book edited by Childs and Reston.

[4] The eleven chapters are "The Dilemma of Liberal Democracy," "The Challenge of Modernity," "The Public and Its Role," "Men and Citizens," "The Public Philosophy," "The Tensions of Constitutionalism," "American Political Institutions," "The Role of Government," "The Pattern of Society," "Leadership," and "The Essential Lippmann."

books. The premise underlying the organization and selection of the relatively brief quotations seems to be that Lippmann, like Hobbes or Montesquieu, has held to certain positions on the major issues of political theory throughout his extraordinary career with no major changes of assumption, reasoning, or conclusion.

This assumption, applicable as it is to most political theorists, even to those who sometimes modified their news on particular points or issues, is completely incorrect and misleading when applied to Lippmann's books of political philosophy. A central argument of this book is that there are five distinct points of view, in assumptions, in methods, and in conclusions, in the nine books here dealt with. I do not argue that my classification is the only possible one. I do believe that it is based firmly on Lippmann's books on political theory published between 1913 and 1955. In them we can follow him as he moves from an optimistic version of Theodore Roosevelt's (and Herbert Croly's) progressivism to serious and searching doubts about the nature and role of public opinion, from a brief, almost casual demotion of government to the role of broker or mediator to a virtually unqualified enthusiasm for the first two years of the New Deal, then to a characterization of that attempt to overcome the economic and social hardships of the greatest of American depressions as a dangerous step toward the loss of liberty and constitutional government, and, finally, in continuance of that thesis, to a nostalgic defense of the glories of free trade, civility, and natural law as they were accepted in the eighteenth century.

So far as I can see, the only ties that bind the five sets of premises, kinds of reasoning, and conclusions together are the common authorship, Lippmann's engaging style, and his apparent conviction in each book or pair of books that he has discovered and is providing a generalized map of the promised land. Previous visits to that land are rarely referred to.

Because of the changes and amazing variety in these books on political theory, I shall take up in chronological order each of the nine books and attempt to outline and summarize them fairly and accurately, as far as this is possible in chapters averaging less than a tenth of the length of the books, with such comments as relate to the book under consideration, reserving to a final chapter a more systematic analysis of the varied character and argument of Lippmann's political theory over a time span of forty-two years.

Walter Lippmann was born in New York on September 23, 1889. Dr. Carl Binger, who was his boyhood schoolmate and friend, relates his upper-middle-class background, the fact that he was a precocious only child, his early distinction as a student ("I don't suppose that he has ever got less than an A on any examination in his life").[5] He was a member of the class of 1910 at Harvard, one that had more than its share of the exceptionally talented, among them T. S. Eliot, Robert Edmond Jones, Heywood Broun, and Jack Reed. He completed the work for his degree in three years but remained a fourth year to study with George Santayana, William James, and Graham Wallas, a visiting lecturer, whose *Human Nature in Politics* had been published in 1908. The book was to have a distinct influence on one period of Lippmann's theory of politics. It is significant of the impression Lippmann made on older men already well known for their achievements that Wallas's next book, *The Great Society* (1914), was dedicated to Walter Lippmann, "in the hope that it may be of some help when you write that sequel to your *Preface to Politics* for which all your friends are looking."

At Harvard Lippmann was interested primarily in philosophy. It was a brilliant department in those days. He did some work with underprivileged children, helped found the Social Politics Club, and was for a time active in the Socialist Club, of which he became president. The socialism of his youth was evidently a very moderate variety, having little resemblance to the revolutionary doctrines of Marx and Engels and no close kinship with

[5] Carl Binger, "A Child of the Enlightenment," in Childs and Reston (eds.), *Walter Lippmann and His Times*, p. 23.

that espoused by the leading American socialist of that age,
Eugene V. Debs. After college he was briefly secretary to the
socialist mayor of Schenectady, George R. Lunn. This lasted but
four months. Lippmann apparently discovered that he had no
taste for the grubbiness of electoral politics or for the views of
those calling themselves socialists. Doctrinaire Marxism he particularly disliked. For a longer period he was with Lincoln Steffens,
then one of the most widely read muckrakers, as Theodore Roosevelt had inappropriately called them. Steffens found Lippmann
all he had hoped for and more, "keen, quiet, industrious," a skill-
ful investigator, a brilliant writer.[6] After a short time in periodical
journalism, Lippmann wrote his first book, followed a year later
by the second. In 1914 he was one of the group that founded *The
New Republic*. Then came a break in which journalism and the
writing of books gave way to government service during the
First World War. He probably had some part in formulating
Wilson's Fourteen Points; he received a commission in military
intelligence and was sent to France to participate in reporting
back to Colonel House and serving on the latter's staff at the Paris
peace negotiations. That experience discouraged, perhaps dis-
illusioned, Lippmann. He resigned and returned to America to
take up the role of critic and counselor, a role he followed, in one
way or another, for nearly half a century. For several years he
was with the *New York World* as editorial writer, head of the
editorial staff, then editor. During that time the *World* was
probably the most stimulating newspaper in America. Its editorials and the page opposite the editorial page were read, talked
about, envied.[7] When the *World* was sold in 1931, he became
a syndicated columnist for the *New York Herald-Tribune*. It was
as a columnist, first in New York, then writing from Washington,
and, finally, for a brief time, from New York again, that he became most widely known and most influential. He was read,

[6] Lincoln Steffens, *Autobiography*, vol. II, ch. 32, esp. pp. 593–594.
[7] On Lippmann and the *World*, see Allen Nevins in Childs and Reston
(eds.), *Walter Lippmann and His Times*, pp. 60–81.

listened to, taken seriously. For more than three decades he was probably the most important writer among the journalists of that time. It was also during that time that he wrote the most widely read of his books on political theory, or, as he finally came to call it, public philosophy.

Five Public Philosophies of
WALTER LIPPMANN

1. The Age of Youthful Optimism

A Preface to Politics

The *Preface to Politics*[1] was published in 1913 shortly after the election of 1912. Lippmann, only three years out of Harvard, was barely twenty-three when it appeared. Though it is a product of the Progressive movement, it is, like Herbert Croly's *Promise of American Life*, which was published four years earlier, far from uncritical when dealing with many reforms and reformers. He was by no means an unqualified worshiper of the voice of the people or of government by and for the common man. But he was an optimist, though his hopes were based upon the exceptional, rather than the average, citizen.

It is a little surprising to read, in a book written in 1912–1913—just after Theodore Roosevelt's great third-party effort, and the year in which Debs's Socialist party received the largest share of

[1] See the bibliography for both original and paperback editions.

the popular vote any party of the left ever polled—that "the most incisive comment on politics to-day is indifference" even among the most intelligent.[2] The first chapter carries on this attitude. It is called "Routineer and Inventor." Lippmann had little sympathy for the American superstition that politics is a conflict between men who represent good and evil. The real distinction is between men who look on government as simply a prescribed course of administration, a matter of routine, and those who look on government as creative problem-solving. Many of the "tinkering reformer[s]" of the good government movement make matters worse. Often they are the "worst of routineers."[3] Conservatives are not the only routineers, and utopia-makers are largely useless.

The statesmen admired by young Lippmann find the institutions and systems of organized society of value, not in and of themselves, but as instruments to carry out human purposes and to serve human need. Those leaders are to be valued who serve "the ideals of human feelings," who initiate, rather than follow mechanical routine. These are "the natural leaders of men."[4]

The introductory pages are stimulating, if not particularly original. That Lippmann had spent more time on philosophy than on the history of the United States Constitution and the relevant *Federalist* essays becomes clear when he says that our Constitution "is a striking example of this machine conception of government. . . . a machine which would preserve its balance without the need of taking human nature into account." The fathers had, he believed, only "a speaking acquaintance," whatever that is, "with humanity." "They worked with the philosophy of their age," which apparently was a compound of Montesquieu and Newton. Had they written in the fire of their youth, they might have made the Constitution more democratic. It is unlikely that they would have made it less mechanical.[5]

The authors of the Constitution were, of course, inventors of

<hr />

2 Walter Lippmann, *A Preface to Politics*, introduction (n.p.).
3 Ibid., pp. 4, 7.
4 Ibid., pp. 8–12.
5 Ibid., pp. 13–15.

the first order, not routineers. They were neither bleeding-heart democrats nor, in any sense appropriate to their time, reactionaries. They drew upon history and upon their study of man's experience in government of, to use Graham Wallas's title, *Human Nature in Politics*. Lippmann, a few pages later, remarks that "human nature is a rather shocking affair if you come to it with ordinary romantic optimism." The founders of the American republic held no such conceptions. They were frank in writing of the folly and wickedness of mankind. They were also cautious, if inventive, optimists.[6]

Lippmann's low opinion of the political thinking of his nation's founders, a view he was later to reverse, is exceeded by his disillusionment with contemporary socialism. The Socialist party is "perhaps the greatest surviving example of the desire to offset natural leadership by artificial contrivance." Its fatal defect is apparently that it does not provide for the natural succession of political forms, anticipate society's needs, or prepare for the prospect of economic expansion.[7]

The tendency is to preserve old forms, to seek for "mere order," to enshrine legalism. The leaders of today are disconcerted by ideas; the great failing of the time is not corruption (as the muckrakers usually saw it), but "lack of insight." What we desperately need is greater concern for the forces of politics, emphasis not on forms but on man's needs. "Statecraft must make human nature its basis. . . . its chief task is the invention of forms and institutions which satisfy the inner needs of mankind." Indeed the true measure of achievement is human happiness.[8] This sounds much like the doctrine of the English Utilitarians, with their pleasure-pain standard of values, but Lippmann believed them to be mechanical in their thinking and limited by a rationalism that failed to take into account the true nature of man.

---

[6] Ibid., p. 39. I have discussed this in the introduction to the John Harvard Library edition of *The Federalist* (Cambridge, 1961) and earlier in "The Federalist on Nature of Man," *Ethics* 70, no. 2 (1949): 1–31.

[7] Lippmann, *Preface to Politics*, pp. 16, 27.

[8] Ibid., pp. 59, 79–84, 86, 90.

For former President Theodore Roosevelt, he had high regard. Taft failed and Bryan was the voice of "confused emotion." Roosevelt "was the first president who shared a new social vision." His first impression of Woodrow Wilson is less clear. Wilson has a clear and flexible mind, but "his contact with American life is not direct"; he is the intellectual in politics but he "belongs among the statesmen," even though limited by "an inability to interpret adequately the world they govern."[9]

Political psychology is not yet mature and certain, but we cannot wait until it is fully developed. We may be "densely ignorant both of man and of politics," but we must nevertheless "put man at the center of politics." That pair of statements calls for clarification, but Lippmann does not pause to reconcile them. He goes on to say that all the great political thinkers since Plato have done this. How then should we change from the method of more than two thousand years? It appears that traditionally, from Plato to the end of the nineteenth century, political man was a dogma; "we must leave him an hypothesis. . . . our task is to temper speculation with scientific humility." The scientific attitude must be "experimental towards life: then every mistake will contribute towards knowledge."[10] We are not told how mistakes are to be determined, or how this triumph of optimism is to be reconciled with popular government or, for that matter, with the maintenance of a minimum and essential degree of order or, as he was later to believe, with the rule of law.

In 1912–1913 Lippmann had almost as low a view of lawyers as that found in the Massachusetts Body of Liberties of 1641, and only less bloody a view than that of Jack Cade. "We have," he asserts, "handed over the government of a nation of people to a set of lawyers, to a class of men who deal in the most verbal and unreal of all human attainments." Apparently government by lawyers is not incompatible with a government based upon elections. The quantitative method of democracy may not always pro-

9 Ibid., pp. 98–100, 102–103.
10 Ibid., pp. 106, 107.

duce wise results, but the results of elections should be heeded, for elections record public opinion; democracy, which to this extent heeds popular sentiment, is therefore "an enlightened form of government." Democrats do not have to believe in the infallibility of the people's choice; "some of us are always in the minority and not a little proud of that distinction." For voting does not tap the wisdom of the people but provides wisdom about the people. Thus belief in democracy rests on solid ground: the wisdom of leaders must be approved by the democracy. "In a rough way and with many exceptions, democracy compels law to approximate human need."[11] It is not clear where this leaves us, as far as giving power and position to lawyers is concerned, but it is evident that the young Lippmann continued to have faith in the democratic tradition and even in the processes of democracy.

His view is not, however, the traditional view of constitutional democracy. In the chapter entitled "Some Necessary Iconoclasm," he argues that "the vital part of the population has pretty well emerged from any dumb acquiescence in constitutions. Theodore Roosevelt, who reflects so much of America, has very definitely cast down this idol." This characterization of the first Roosevelt is reminiscent of one by Justice Holmes, who wrote in a letter to Sir Frederick Pollock that, according to "a Senator, what the boys like about Roosevelt is that he doesn't care a damn for the law." Lippmann thought Roosevelt "some twenty years behind the pioneer and about six months ahead of the majority." His ability to stand so close, though ahead of the majority, gives us assurance that this "much-needed iconoclasm is in process of achievement." If the mechanical limitations of constitutionalism are on the way out, so are "the Sanctity of Private Property, Vested Rights, Competition the Life of Trade, Prosperity (at any cost)." The "early maxims of capitalism are doomed."[12]

[11] Ibid., pp. 113, 115, 116. This brief discussion is probably the nearest Lippmann ever came to a theory of democracy that involves a principle of political obligation applicable to all citizens.

[12] Ibid., pp. 184–185. For Justice Holmes's estimate of Theodore Roosevelt, see *Holmes-Pollock Letters*, ed. Mark Howe, II, 63–64.

What Lippmann wrote in 1912–1913 about law, constitutional-ism, and classical economics must have made him blush for the errors of his youth a generation later, but some of the pages that follow those just summarized foreshadow his analysis in *Public Opinion* (1922). Thus, the great weakness of American journalism is not to be found in control by men of wealth, but in the prej-udices of "the great mass of average citizens (to which none of us belongs)." Because of these prejudices "American journalism is flaccid, so repetitious and so dull." The will of the people "should be the law of the land. But it is a caricature of democracy to make it also the law of individual initiative." We must not pro-pose what is immediately acceptable. It is not for politics to pre-scribe the "ultimate values" of life; the business of politics is to rid us of oppression and to expand the possibilities for happi-ness.[13] That is not a meager objective for politics, especially in view of the limitations the author has pointed out.

Having read the history of political theory, looking mistakenly for what will never be found—"an absolutely true philosophy of politics"—Lippmann decided that we cannot expect that anyone "has done the world's thinking once and for all." That a body or system of theory might be adequate for one time and place and in-appropriate for others seems not to have occurred to him, though he does go on to say that "political philosophy at once appears as a human invention in a particular crisis—an instrument to fit the need. The pretension to finality falls away."[14]

The remaining third of the book is primarily a plea to base political decisions upon the observation of human nature, which has changed "very little . . . since our Western wisdom has come to be recorded."[15] Apparently Lippmann thought that he was advocating something new and important. He was reacting against the curiously dry rationalism of the later nineteenth cen-tury, as was his teacher, Graham Wallas, in *Human Nature in*

[13] Lippmann, *Preface to Politics*, pp. 197, 201.
[14] Ibid., pp. 205, 209.
[15] Ibid., p. 210.

Politics. Of course, what Wallas and Lippmann wrote in 1908 and 1913 was what James Madison had repeatedly asserted in his *Federalist* essays. Both Madison and John Adams thought that human nature was a constant, at least in the recorded history of the West, and they never would have disagreed with Lippmann's declaration that "the one thing that no democrat may assume is that the people are all dear good souls, fully competent for their task."[16] They, along with the other founders, did believe that in a properly constructed republic popular government could be successful. Lippmann's ringing declaration concerning the nature of political man was worth repeating in 1913, as in most other times, even if it was not original and had not been neglected by the founders of the American republic. Similarly, there was no harm in asserting that statesmanship "must find popular feeling, organize it, and make that the motive power of government,"[17] though he was not so aware of the problem of minority feelings and rights in 1913 as we have become since about 1919.

It is not completely clear what meaning he attaches to some

16 Ibid., p. 302. Charles A. Beard's *Economic Interpretation of the Constitution* was published the same year as *A Preface to Politics.* It led many scholars to read *The Federalist* more carefully, especially Madison's number 10, though the result generally was an exaggerated emphasis upon economic motives that obscured other motives behind political behavior. (See n. 6 *supra.*) In his sixth essay in the greatest of American arguments for specific action (ratification), Hamilton wrote of "the imperfections, weaknesses, and evils incident to society in every shape," and in the thirty-seventh Madison echoed him on the infirmities and depravities of the human character. Madison's observation in the tenth essay is even more perceptive, and shows a maturity of understanding that Lippmann, for all his emphasis upon the importance of human nature, rarely equaled: "So strong is this propensity of mankind to fall into mutual animosities, that where no substantial occasion presents itself, the most frivolous and fanciful distinctions have been sufficient to kindle their unfriendly passions and excite their most violent conflicts." Jefferson wrote in 1788 that *The Federalist* was "the best commentary on the principles of government which ever was written" (*Writings,* ed. Ford, V, 83). From this estimate he never changed. Many years later he listed it as one of the four writings to be read by all the students at the University of Virginia.

17 Lippmann, *Preface to Politics,* p. 220.

of the other broad generalizations of these pages. For example, myths are to be judged "by their ability to express aspirations," and "reforms are . . . to be applied when by experiment they show their civilizing value."[18] Nor is it clear why the primary issues are not "the tariff, the trusts, the currency, and electoral machinery"; they were not, as we know in retrospect, insignificant issues. Lippmann is less than specific when he says that we need a government "which provides most," one which furnishes a "civilized environment," one which is less a policeman and more a "producer."[19]

The important and indeed essential question is how we achieve these admirable objectives. Here, Lippmann is vague. He appears to favor the Continental multiparty system, with its ampler reflection of desires, needs, and ideas, a system that has not always, especially before 1939, been spectacularly successful in producing enough stability to make possible continuing emphasis on the needs and desires of the people. He even suggests a revision of the legislative body to include one house that candidly reflects and represents special interests.[20] These are, however, passing comments or suggestions and are not developed.

The final chapter, "Revolution and Culture," is a youthful tour de force, a collection of generalizations remarkable for inclusiveness and sweeping vagueness rather than as a map to the new age of profound and necessary changes.[21] Thus, we read in this chapter that "we are not civilized enough to meet an issue before it becomes acute," that "paternalism is not dependable," even if, and that is not certain, "desirable." He writes of the "unimaginative greed and endless stupidity of the dominant classes," almost as though he were still president of the Harvard Socialist Club. But the chapter is not clearly an indictment of the "dominant classes," whatever they are, for he is more concerned that states-

18 Ibid., pp. 228, 243.
19 Ibid., pp. 255–271 passim.
20 Ibid., pp. 260–261, 264.
21 Ibid., pp. 272–318.

men foresee the causes and needs that result in crises, and that they not neglect man in their concern with institutions.[22] "Constitutions do not make people; people make constitutions." Real statesmanship, therefore, "begins by accepting human nature," though this does not mean that "we accept its present character." Ninety pages earlier he seemed to say that human nature had remained unchanged throughout the record of western history. Now we do not, apparently, have to accept it as it is, presumably because the true statesman can choose between "cruelty and lust" at one period and the "richest values of civilized life" at another, for his task is to "provide fine opportunities for the expression of human impulses."[23]

We are not told how this objective is to be attained or carried out, other than by never forgetting that the stuff of politics is human nature, as most politicians and political philosophers have been aware since Socrates. But he is certain that not all people are "dear good souls" and that "no amount of charters, direct primaries, and short ballots will make a democracy out of an illiterate people."[24] There was probably too great an emphasis on reforms in the machinery of government in 1912, as Roosevelt's Progressive platform indicates, but there was also a widespread movement to eradicate illiteracy, as there had been for a century.

It is easy to be critical of this book written by an optimistic young man whose talent was as apparent as his limitations. He thought himself a thoroughgoing realist, though his experience and his knowledge of history was inadequate for the formulation of a truly realistic theory of politics. It was a promising book, as Graham Wallas saw, and its final sentence is illustrative of its time: "For the age is rich with varied and generous passions."[25]

[22] Ibid., pp. 278, 279, 283.
[23] Ibid., p. 298.
[24] Ibid., p. 305.
[25] Ibid., p. 318. On page 306 he had written that "without a favorable culture political schemes are a mere imposition. They will not work without people to work them."

Drift and Mastery

Lippmann's second book is a sequel to the first. Whether this sequel was what Graham Wallas and Lippmann's many admirers hoped for is today unimportant. In it there is much the same insistent emphasis on being scientific and realistic. There is a greater faith in the future, an unhesitating willingness not to be bound by the past, by traditions, or even by accepted views of the rights of property.

The point of view that most clearly characterizes the book is found sixty-eight pages from the end: the only tenable position today is one that looks to the future. "America is preëminently the country where there is practical substance in Nietzsche's advice that we should live not for our fatherland, but for our children's land." The great problem is "to substitute purpose for tradition." To achieve this will be to effect one of the most profound changes in all history. Life can no longer be dealt with as an inheritance from the past. "We have to deal with it deliberately, devise its social organization, alter its tools, formulate its methods, educate and control it. In endless ways ... break up routines, make decisions, choose our ends, select means."[26]

Even Plato's guardians did not have the power to attempt what Lippmann proposes in this extraordinarily optimistic statement. But Lippmann was, at this time, under the influence of the progressive impulse. The largely unconscious creed of progress, inherited from the nineteenth century, had not been wrecked by the First World War and by the failure to achieve at Versailles what men in high office often called a "just and lasting peace."

The spirit of the book is very much akin to Theodore Roosevelt's New Nationalism and the Progressive platform of 1912. The former president wrote a highly favorable review of it, together with Herbert Croly's *Progressive Democracy*, in the *Outlook*.[27] In a letter Roosevelt remarked that Lippmann is "on the

[26] Walter Lippmann, *Drift and Mastery*, pp. 266–267.
[27] Arthur Schlesinger, "Walter Lippmann: The Intellectual v. Politics," in

whole the most brilliant young man of his age in all the United States. He is a great writer and economist."[28]

Lippmann's hopes for the future are less qualified than they had been only a year before. In the last paragraph of the book he writes almost lyrically of the vision of the present, so much clearer than that of the rebels of the nineteenth century. To be sure, it is still "murky, fragmentary, and distorted" when compared with the vision we need. But we are more accustomed to freedom than were our predecessors. We can face life naturally, free from the bogeys of the past; we can deal with reality free from superstition.[29]

In the 350 pages or thereabouts (for the introduction of 16 pages should not be omitted), Lippmann is freer with criticisms of what has been done or proposed than he is ready to propose a program or even a set of principles making the best use of the new freedom. There are, however, some suggestions scattered along the way. Thus, in the first paragraph of the introduction he points out that the widespread unemployment in New York in early 1914 gave the anarchists an exceptional opportunity for agitation, and the newspapers and police reacted with hysteria, clubbing, and arrests. When a new police commissioner changed the policy from official lawlessness to the full right for the anarchists to express their grievances, the anarchists were thrown off guard. It became necessary for them to propose solutions, and they had none. So in the United States, we are a bewildered, immature democracy, with no tyrant to attack. It is not enough to speak with rhetorical extravagance about the people's will. It is no longer profitable to attack the evils of the plutocracy, for our failings

---

Lippmann and His Times, ed. Marquis Childs and James Reston, pp. 196–197. Croly's book also appeared in 1914.

[28] Theodore Roosevelt, *Letters*, ed. Elting E. Morison and John M. Blum, VIII, 872.

[29] Lippmann, *Drift and Mastery*, p. 334. A large part of this book is so at odds with Lippmann's later writings that it is easy to understand why few of its characteristic statements, as well as few from *The Method of Freedom*, are included in *The Essential Lippmann*.

are not in the strength of the older order but in the floundering, clouded vision of the democracy that we have. A nation of uncritical drifters can do little. Democracy "is a weapon in the hands of those who have the courage and the skill to wield it; in all others it is a rusty piece of junk."[30]

Since we inherit a tradition of change and progress, since the businessman is no longer an infallible authority and the sacredness of private property is no longer unquestioned, the real problem is how business methods are to be altered. Only the very ignorant desire to preserve our economic system in its existing form. This means that the battle is less against surviving prejudice than against the chaotic conditions of a newer and more open freedom. We do not need utopias or even inclusive and final programs, much less blueprints. This book begins "with the obvious drift of our time and gropes for the conditions of mastery."[31]

Chapter 1 deals with the muckrakers, those who exposed corruption, dishonesty, and bribery, first among politicians, then among the "malefactors of great wealth," to use Theodore Roosevelt's phrase. We know far more than we did before about the sad state of some political leaders and organizations, as well as about the methods by which clever and not too scrupulous businessmen raided their competitors or milked railroads and banks. Lippmann's conclusion at this point seems to be that there has always been corruption in politics, but that it was not a cause for great concern so long as the activities of government were limited.[32] This explanation does not go very far toward explaining the corruption, which reached well beyond the expansion of functions in towns, cities, counties, and states, especially when there were sudden increases in population, sometimes due to greatly increased immigration.

What is perhaps most important about the exposés of corruption

---

[30] Ibid., p. xvii.

[31] Ibid., p. xxiv. On page xxv there is an almost, if not quite, unique favorable reference to Jefferson (along with Marx and Lincoln). This is curiously inconsistent with the critical citation of Jefferson in A Preface to Politics.

[32] Ibid., p. 19.

in government and business is that new standards are being developed, amounting to a revolutionary change in business motives and to recognition of "the emerging power of labor and the consumer."[33]

In general, Lippmann agrees with Roosevelt rather than with Brandeis about the surge toward increasing size in business.[34] Government can be just as efficient as private enterprise if the same degree of authority is vested in those who manage, as was demonstrated in the construction of the Panama Canal,[35] and some large-scale enterprises, such as railroads, may become government owned. Government bonds could be a safer investment than corporate stocks, and the stockholders of the great corporations have no control over management. This line of reasoning leads Lippmann to a conclusion exceedingly surprising to those who know his views only as they are set forth in *The Good Society* and *The Public Philosophy*.

After remarking that no man in his right mind wants to change the economy so as to decrease its productivity, he casually writes, five pages later, that the "time may come, I am inclined to think it is sure to come, when the government will be operating the basic industries, railroads, mines, and so forth."[36] The standard to be used is apparently not whether socialism of this kind is correct by the conventional principles of economic theory, but whether men can develop industrial systems that operate without the need of paying rent or interest. The economists' measure of motives in terms of money conceals a vicious circle of reasoning; they say little more than "whatever is, is necessary; [and] then, adding insult to incompetence, [they] infer that whatever is, is right."[37]

There is no validity to the argument that we lack the wealth to pay for democracy. We do not. It is entirely possible for us to

[33] Ibid., p. 25.
[34] Ibid., pp. 35–49.
[35] Ibid., p. 62.
[36] Ibid., pp. 107, 113.
[37] Ibid., pp. 119–120.

meet the demands of labor and the needs of consumers, to under-
take the programs of social reform that would restore dignity to
"our sooty life." To be sure, it would require the curtailment of
wasteful practices, a far more efficient use of natural, human, and
technological resources. All this can be achieved if there is constant pressure from those who work in the industrial system.

Clearly, at this time, Lippmann was not disturbed at the prospect of government ownership of major industry and of a large
portion of the land, but he thought the antitrust legislation and
the various attempts at enforcement, including the Supreme
Court's invention of the rule of reason, stupid and destructive.
We cannot return to the old life of villages, small farms, and
small business. Bryan was fighting for the old simplicities of
agrarian society already doomed by the larger economy of the
modern era. "He is the true Don Quixote of our politics, for he
moves in a world that has ceased to exist."[38] He did, however,
speak for a great force in America. The various forms of that
force made a majority, leading to the disruption of the Republican
party, to much of the strength of both Progressives and Socialists
in 1912, and to the victory of Wilson, though he was not a part
of the power that elected him. Wilson dreams of an older world
that he knows is passing into history. Here again Lippmann dis-
agrees with the Brandeis dream of small units of business and
agrees with Roosevelt and Croly. The intelligent men of today
should not confine themselves to small-scale enterprise of the
traditional kind.   The great opportunity is that of "industrial
statesmanship," of giving order and direction to business activity.
These men have been trained to a simpler life, often to the village
ideal, but they must abandon that ideal, that way of life, and in-
vent ways of dealing with the scale of economic enterprise that
machinery has made inevitable.[39]

Among the institutions standing in the way of finding solutions
to existing problems are the courts. The result is that defective

[38] Ibid., pp. 121–125, 129, 130.
[39] Ibid., pp. 141–148.

sociology of judges and their economic prejudices are destroying the prestige of the bench. They have great power and they use it by making law that applied a generation or more ago, not the law required by modern necessities.[40]

In the political structure of our government there are other obstacles. The regulation of the trusts is made difficult by the fact that states are too small and the nation often too large to get the job done. For many purposes the natural geographic regions would be more effective units of control. We cannot allow the national government all the power necessary for proper control, yet the states have been unsuccessful in their attempts to regulate business. Here we must contrive to suit governmental needs and procedures to the needs of the present day; we must not be bound by the ideas of the eighteenth century. This involves, among other things, recognition of many kinds of organizations, such as labor unions, which are not official or governmental. The adjustment of these unofficial sovereignties "to each other [and to official governments] is a task for which political science is not prepared." The improvement of labor unions—not their abolition, but creation of a sense of responsibility—is as essential as creating a sufficient number of businessmen. This cannot be done by decree. But then all these problems and needs are part of the complexity of the task of democracy, elements in a system that grew up so quickly and unexpectedly that men were not only caught completely unprepared, but even now cannot grasp its complexity or predict its future. Old precedents are no longer adequate guides, since we face new facts. There is no single, central authority to serve as a guide or lead; accepted rules of conduct have lost their meaning. Man needs guides in his political and economic life, but changes distract him when he most needs such aides. And "the more advanced he is, the more he flounders."[41]

A few years later such generalizations brought gloom and despair to Lippmann. In the years of his youth (he was barely twenty-five when this book appeared), he saw them as a challenge

40 Ibid., pp. 158–162.
41 Ibid., p. 170.

to leave off the old, including the one-shot reforms, and to win mastery through intelligent and persistent effort.

In the chapter that follows, not very accurately labeled "Drift," he begins by remarking that even the "New Freedom" assumes that our early form of democracy is retrievable. It is, in fact, altogether self-deluding to wish to return to that age, which was neither golden nor democratic, in which, for example, even the most peaceful trade union was illegal and suffrage was limited. The American dream of the past is based upon myth and a longing for the belief that natural man was good.

All this is as illusory as a belief in the certainties of evolution, in the inevitability of progress. Such dreams are found in various forms, including the old-fashioned Marxist determinism. Its adherents are not genuine revolutionaries, for they merely place their faith in the unfolding of a plan, sketches of which are in their possession as a result of the labors of Karl Marx. "They are the interested pedants of destiny. They are God's audience, and they know the plot so well that occasionally they prompt Him."[42] At the time Lippmann wrote, American Marxists probably numbered no more than a few thousands. Debs, the Socialist leader who received the largest proportion of votes of any candidate of the left, was only partly a Marxist. Lippmann, who sees the Socialist party as inconsistently Marxist, finds that this party has been unable to work out a viable political program.

Since Lippmann has little more of interest to say of the party of Debs and his successors, it may be remarked that they never did succeed in developing a usable or valuable political platform, one adapted to the needs and the ideas of the United States, partly, at least, because their political theory was either largely alien or adapted from other minor progressive or liberal parties.

Lippmann disposes almost as summarily of other one-charge solutions: votes for women, the short ballot, a democratic constitution, the single tax, syndicalism. Some of these proposals have value, but generally they are almost as useless as vacillating in-

42 Ibid., p. 182.

decision. Such proposals share with indecision a failure to grasp the reality of what is possible. One thinks of Irving Babbitt and Paul Elmer More, who say that certitude was destroyed together with absolute authority by the French Revolution, and propose to remedy the situation by turning back to the "eternal forms of justice and moderation." All this is a waste of effort and results in drift. Once liberty has been established, the real work begins. Those who set us free left us to find our own way.[43]

The liberal faith lacks the calm of absolutes. It cannot be compared to the Rock of Gibraltar. "We have to be exuberant and conquering to rejoice in change." There is a general decline of authority in religion, in politics, in community. But we will not be both free and strong until we "find within ourselves" the standards and the procedures with which to take advantage of our opportunities.[44]

If the enlargement and ferment of the modern world have robbed absolutism of its excuse, if the old sanctities of private property are gone and the present situation seems full of peril, this is because we can no longer speak of "eternal principles of conduct" as though we still lived in simple village society. We must realize that in the conditions of our time, with a continent being exploited by people of many races, a decade brings many changes, a generation a whole new way of life. The new world is not so comfortable as the old, or as what the old has been thought to be, but it is more challenging. Sharper thinking is required because repose is gone and with it reliance upon ancient creeds. We are all spiritual immigrants and we cannot lean upon authority.[45]

In the next chapter, "A Note on the Woman's Movement," the author foresaw so many changes in the status of women that have now come to pass that much of the chapter is dated, but he just as clearly sees that many problems will remain to be solved or worked at. The women's movement sets an example of the cooperation that can lay "the real foundations for the modern world."

[43] Ibid., pp. 195–197.
[44] Ibid., pp. 202, 206.
[45] Ibid., pp. 206–211.

A people will need to be trained to use these foundations, these possibilities. The old patriarchal family structure is giving way to a feminism that offers great hope for the future.[46]

Fears of the unknown, the bogeys, are usually excessive, sometimes hysterical, and generally have little foundation. Exorcising these fears is integral to the success of self-government. Much political discussion, especially political agitation, consists of finding scapegoats. Consequently, we are constantly beset by "timidities and panics, distorting superstitions." One of the main causes of drift in leaders is the imaginary evils they construct. The timidities and conflicts that once found refuge in religion must now give way to a disciplined new strength. It is not enough to exorcise the bogeys; the terrors of fact remain. We must build up a clear conception of the real world. This will not be easy, for as yet we have only a vague notion of the possibilities of democratic culture. It is far easier to destroy absolutism than to master the possibilities of the future.[47]

In the United States the quality of life has in great measure been raised above the level of the primitive. This has given some basis for our historical optimism. Our past mistakes have not been fatal. We have scarcely begun to draw on our immense wealth. For these reasons America continues to hold out the best hope for a democratic society. Our first goal, if we are to achieve the aims of self-government, must be to lift all men "above the misery line." We must fulfill this "most elementary duty of the democratic state," not only because the abjectly deprived suffer great misery, but also because their festering discontent is the "poison" of the democracy. With nothing to lose, these people fall easy victim to debasement, deception, and demagoguery. No modern state can stand on the treacherous foundation of dire poverty and subjection. Everyone must have some stake and some hope for the future.

As we seek the end of poverty, so we seek the end of another

---

[46] Ibid., ch. XI (pp. 212–239), particularly pp. 238, 239.
[47] Ibid., pp. 244–250.

prop of absolutism, the traditional emphasis upon chastity. We do not wish for promiscuity, for either Don Juan or ascetics, but for a sane attitude toward sex and toward the responsibilities of parents. The church, standing opulent in the midst of poverty and offering spiritual reward for renunciation of the world and the flesh, required obedience because the other two props failed. It is not surprising that defenders of authority hold labor unions and feminism as their deadly enemies.

Pragmatism, judging by results rather than by authority, is not invariably and always possible. One should, for example, follow the orders of his physician. We do not seek the complete substitution of pragmatism for authority, only that the ideal be tested in the real world. Modern virtues reverse the old authoritarian ones. The greatest good is no longer to be found in renunciation of this world; we seek instead the fullest development of human potential and of the earth's resources. The goal of democracy is "the richest life that men can devise for themselves."[48]

There follow the paragraphs summarized at the beginning of this section: the substitution of purpose for tradition, of mastery for drift. After those hopeful and ambitious statements we are told of the importance of the subconscious, the role of the nonrational, the accidental, the achievements that were not the result of clearly thought out intentions. This apparently offers further reason for more scientific procedures, even to "learning to control the inventor." Democratic politics is closely akin to scientific thinking. "As absolutism falls, science arises. It *is* self-government."[49] Twenty or thirty years later, Lippmann, with the examples of Germany and Japan before him, would have been less certain of the results of science and learning.

At this time Lippmann had no fear of science or any conception of two cultures that do not meet and sometimes even conflict. Instead he sees science as the underpinning of the attitude that is self-governing and most adequately named humanistic. It is the "foe of bogeys, and, therefore, a method of laying the conflict of

48 Ibid., p. 263.
49 Ibid., pp. 273, 275.

the soul." A half-century later it is almost as surprising as it is interesting to read, in words written by a young and very promising humanist, that "the scientific spirit is the discipline of democracy, the escape from drift, the outlook of a free man. Its direction is to distinguish fact from fancy; its 'enthusiasm is for the possible'; its promise is the shaping of fact to a chastened and honest dream."[50]

This is not the end of Lippmann's youthful praise of the scientific spirit. He links it to the goal common to all men everywhere. Only its discipline promises that different men, looking at the same group of facts, will arrive at similar conclusions. Science is "the discipline of democracy. No omnipotent rules can deal with our world, nor the scattered anarchy of individual temperaments. Mastery is inevitably a matter of cooperation."[51] We must, like the Greek philosophers, concentrate on what man ought to do to make human life more valuable, not on what he ought not to do. Conservatives may ridicule the "futurist habit of mind," for it is always easy to find fault with enthusiasts, but this hope in the future is not mere fad. Though the hopes of the optimists, those who welcome change, even progress, have not yet been precisely formulated, their faith should be taken seriously, not condemned. Critics must try to comprehend them as only a beginning.[52]

The final chapter of the book contains a reiteration and restatement of these ideas. Lippmann does not commit himself to any one of the proposed roads to freedom and enlarged satisfaction. He sees faults and limitations in Wilson, Haywood, the suffragettes, the utopians, the Marxists, the classical economists, the bureaucratic dreamers. What is intolerable, however, is not unreal hope, but hidebound traditionalism. We cannot remain content with whatever happens to exist, nor can we flee to a golden age of the past.[53]

The mastery of which he writes will not come about through

---

[50] Ibid., pp. 276, 275.

[51] Ibid., pp. 285–286.

[52] Ibid., pp. 286–288.

[53] Ibid., pp. 289–329. See especially the disparaging remarks on Adam Smith, pp. 307–308.

single-minded pursuit of any exclusive plan. We find "something multitudinous about the very notion of democracy, something that offends our inherited prejudices." Mastery is not to be achieved by adopting a simple formula, for it "is an immense collaboration, in which all the promises of to-day will have their vote."[54] This will not necessitate revolution; it will require continued effort, far more so than the absolutism of castle and church, continued criticism, as well as effort and an affirmative vision.[55]

[54] Ibid., p. 329.

[55] Ibid., pp. 329–334. On the very last page he makes one of his dubious statements about the history of self-government in the United States: "The men who founded democracy were more concerned with the evils of the kingly system than they were with the possibilities of self-government" (ibid., p. 334). Except for Tom Paine, who, to repeat, had little influence on the form and nature of government adopted in state and nation, this is almost completely incorrect.

2. Democracy and the Defects of Public Opinion

Public Opinion

One of the sharpest changes in the political theory of Walter Lippmann took place between the publication of *Drift and Mastery* in 1914 and *Public Opinion* in 1922. How much this was due to his disappointing and disillusioning experience in government service, particularly in the Paris negotiations leading to the Versailles Treaty, how much to his experience as a newspaper man, and how much to the spirit and temper of the times is uncertain. Clearly the attitude of 1922 is a long distance from the buoyancy and enthusiasm of the earlier books. To be sure, there are indications in his youthful writings, particularly in *A Preface to Politics*, that even in the most enlightened democracy most men do not make judgments, or cast their votes, on the basis of calm reflection and after thorough study of the facts involved. He does, however, brush those doubts away with the conclusion that the indifference and comparative ignorance of most citizens can be compensated for by far-seeing and dynamic leaders, such as Theodore Roosevelt. The optimism of the *Preface* is exceeded by that of *Drift and Mastery*, in which there are few of the doubts about the processes of democracy that were in some part a result of the teachings of Graham Wallas's *Human Nature in Politics*. The theme of his second book might be a variant on the song of the movement led by the late Martin Luther King, Jr., only Lippmann's title would be "We Can Overcome."

Public Opinion is not a book to be summed up accurately in a phrase, or even a paragraph. The approach in it, or rather in the first seven of its eight parts, is suggested vividly by the epigraph: the most memorable of the fables or allegories in Plato's *Republic*, the figure of the cave in Book VII. A group of persons have been chained since childhood in an underground cave, a cave whose only opening is behind them. They can never see the persons who pass outside or the objects they carry. Because there is a fire behind the men and animals moving across the entrance to the cave, the prisoners can see only shadows of those who pass by on the wall of the cave. Consequently, they think that the shadows thrown on the wall are the reality. "And if they were able to talk with one another, would they not suppose that they were naming what was actually before them?"

Part I, the introduction, is limited to a single chapter, appropriately entitled "The World Outside and the Pictures in Our Heads." He begins with a story, probably imaginary and certainly allegorical. The time was 1914. Several Englishmen, Frenchmen, and Germans were living on an island in the ocean; their only news of the outside world arrived every two months via the British mail steamer. When the ship appeared in mid-September the islanders learned that their picture of Europe at peace was wrong, that for six weeks those of them who were English and French had been enemies of those who were Germans.[1] Those persons living in the countries at war learned of hostilities more quickly,

---

[1] Walter Lippmann, *Public Opinion*, p. 3.

but there the interval may have been a matter of days, or even hours, instead of weeks.

The point of using Plato's allegory and the tale of the remote islanders is made clear in the first two sentences that follow. If we reflect, we can see how little direct knowledge we have of the environment in which we live. We receive news about it at varying times, but the picture we get is rarely exact. Nor is the "news" when it arrives ordinarily an accurate version of the truth. It is not simply, as Holmes said in his famous speech on Chief Justice Marshall, that "we live by symbols, and what shall be symbolized by an image of the sight depends upon the mind of him who sees it," but that each symbol is far less inclusive because there are so many competing ones.[2] Chief Justice Holmes, in a movingly poetic conclusion to his speech from the bench of the Massachusetts Supreme Judicial Court, had said that Marshall could stand for the glory of his state, for the success of the Union, for the rise of a new body of jurisprudence, for the power and influence of an idea, for the flag. Lippmann, more prosaically, argues that the images or pictures that persons have, either of events or of the personages of his times, are more often than not made up of varying parts of illusion and misinterpretation, with an occasional intrusion of accurate information. One factor is common—between man and the world around him is placed a "pseudo-environment," and man's behavior is governed by his reaction to that fiction. In Justice Holmes's variety of symbols for Marshall, none is misleading; all are accurate, though the emphasis varies depending on the point of view. Lippmann views the symbols to which man reacts as part of a fictitious world that may result in contradiction when men learn the truth by experience, when they experience what Herbert Spencer called the "tragedy of the murder of a Beautiful Theory by a Gang of Brutal Facts." We are more often than not governed in our social life by fictions, though fictions need not be lies. Fictions are simply representations of the environment that vary "from complete hallucination to the scientist's perfectly self-con-

[2] Oliver Wendell Holmes, *Collected Legal Papers*, p. 270; Lippmann, *Public Opinion*, p. 11.

scious use of a schematic model or his decision that for his particular problem accuracy beyond a certain number of decimal places is not important." This is not necessarily error. In fact, because of the size, complexity, and transience of the real environment, we can never adequately comprehend it. Its endlessly changing and subtle variety is beyond our power to know.[3]

In effect, Lippmann is saying that the world we live in and the problems we face cannot be compared to those of the small New England town with its annual town meeting in which there is a direct confrontation between and among leaders and citizens informed and competent to vote on the issues they face. We do not even know how men would act in response to the facts of social life. All that we really know is how they behave in response to what can be called an incomplete picture of society.

Nor do we know with any certainty what motives men have. The class consciousness of Marxism and the pleasure-pain psychology of the Utilitarians both beg the real questions: Why do men decide the way they do? How do they arrive at one moral stance rather than another? What determines their notions of self-interest or success? Neither the Freudians, the conservative critics, nor the romantics face the fact that men necessarily deal with baffling and elusive facts, that what may be a normal environment for the psychologist or the sociologist is in fact his own model substituted for reality.[4]

The world in which we must act politically is too remote and complex for us, since all man gets are a few messages from the outside. Therefore, the theory of the "original democrats" is today unacceptable, and "representative government, either in . . . politics, or in industry, cannot be worked successfully . . . unless there is an independent, expert organization for making the unseen facts intelligible to those who have to make the decisions."[5]

There are several debatable assumptions in those statements. It is perhaps enough to say here that in the first relatively brief sec-

[3] Lippmann, *Public Opinion*, pp. 15, 16.
[4] Ibid., pp. 26–27.
[5] Ibid., pp. 29–31.

tion of *Public Opinion* Lippmann has pretty well undercut the views he himself had expressed in his first two books. The remainder of *Public Opinion* is a development of this introductory section. In it we can find some of Lippmann's most fruitful insights, as well as one of his most disappointing conclusions.

Part II has as its title, "Approaches to the World Outside." The opening pages are the product of the author's experience and observation of wartime censorship and propaganda. These barriers to the truth of what is being done or planned result in a vast disparity between the world outside and the pictures the citizen has of the world. It is not only in time of war, however, that such barriers and such disparities exist. Even an individual of large income, who can travel and can survey at least the surface of the world beyond his neighborhood, is so hedged about with social standards or taboos, with lack of interest, with various inherited and acquired prejudices and conditions that he rarely takes advantage of his opportunities for becoming acquainted with public affairs, with the opportunities for serious or meaningful analysis. We are far too concerned with our own affairs and too much influenced by our preconceived ideas.[6]

The next chapter, "Time and Attention," was written before the day of either radio or television news summaries and commentaries, or, for that matter, of the nationally syndicated newspaper columnist. How greatly they would have influenced Lippmann's conclusions is debatable, but, partly on the basis of some early surveys, partly on the basis of observation, he concludes that, even with the reading of newspapers, magazines, and various organizations and lecture series, none of us devotes much time to getting full information about the unseen environment in which we live.[7]

Apparently, even if much more time and attention were given to reading about or listening to the discussion of public affairs, we would not be much better informed. The distortions in dispatches, the variations in human abilities and concerns and susceptibilities, these and other factors he had not adequately as-

6 Ibid., pp. 35–57 passim.
7 Ibid., pp. 58–63.

sessed in 1913 and 1914, combine with the difficulties of facts themselves to prevent clear and accurate perception. We are, therefore, more influenced by fiction than by fact.

Part III, "Stereotypes," is probably the major section of the book, not so much because the central idea there presented at some length (77 pages) is entirely new as because it is discussed vividly and its relation to the role of public opinion in a self-governing society is more effectively developed than in any preceding book by an American. We all know, if we stop to think about it, that the view depends in some part upon the point of view. In the old bit of doggerel, "Two prisoners looked out from behind the bars; one saw the mud, the other the stars." What Lippmann does brilliantly is to relate this modest truism to the theory of public opinion, or, more accurately, to the assumptions behind the theory expressed in this book. In brief, his argument is that "for the most part we do not first see and then define, we define first and then see. In the great blooming buzzing confusion of the outer world we pick out what our culture has already defined for us, and we tend to perceive that which we have picked out in the form stereotyped for us by our culture."[8]

The connection between what we observe and what the scene encompasses is largely predetermined by the stereotypes in the mind of the observer. We tend to think and to report in terms of labels that oversimplify and distort the reality. Even trained observers cannot be depended upon to give an accurate account of what happens in front of them. The influences forming our stereotypes are many. They begin in infancy and continue through life. Plato's views of the kind of poetry to be presented to future guardians of his state are as clear an example of this conception as is the present-day influence of the stereotypes found in moving pictures. So powerful are the inherited stereotypes, those transmitted from generation to generation, that to most persons of any

[8] Ibid., p. 81. There is an interesting account of a staged moment of melodrama at the Congress of Psychology at Göttingen. Lippmann's conclusion is that a majority of the reports by these professional observers were so inaccurate as to be worthless as evidence (ibid., pp. 82–83).

given clan or class they are accepted as fact. Only a few can learn to discount them and therefore come nearer to accuracy of observation.

Moreover, stereotypes, which allow an economy of effort, also promote a sense of security. They permit us to feel at home, to be members, to fit in. When the stereotypes are attacked, the whole world they represent is shaken, for the stereotypes provide the defense of our tradition and of the position we occupy in society.[9] Of course it is not an ideal world we see through our stereotypes, but a familiar world that will not contradict our expectations. This may include the conceptions represented by such words as "progress" and "perfection." The American stereotype found among those with deeply planted roots and newly arrived immigrant alike is that of mechanical progress. Ours is a religion of success, of expansion—the growth of villages into cities, prosperity, the American way of doing things. There are, of course, changes, cycles in stereotypes, but in its time the stereotype simplifies the business of getting on in the world we live in, protects us from its baffling complexities.[10]

It might seem that Lippmann had made the point that we see what we expect to see, but he had two more chapters and forty pages to add to the argument. Chapter IX, "Codes and Their Enemies," is primarily a discussion of the limitations imposed on us by our very expertise, whether in science, in industry, in a profession, or in love.

Among the specialists who have imposed a point of view on those who follow them are the economists. Finding the social and economic system of their time too complex to describe, they simplified that system into a representation of how capitalism ought to work. The model is a fiction, but it has been accepted as a standard version. At least it was accepted by the successful. The failures and the victims of this economic system were sometimes less convinced. The captains of industry looked on the progress and

9 Ibid., pp. 95–96.
10 Ibid., pp. 104–114.

development of the economy and found it good; those who did not succeed often saw it very differently.[11]

This reference to the disenchantment of the losers in the economic struggle somewhat weakens the continuity of the argument, for the author goes on to cite our many ways of describing the unseen world. No stereotype is neutral; each is a preconception rooted in the passions and prejudices of human nature. Codes of conduct and standards of morality or good taste, which "standardize" these prejudices, are essential, but it is true that they limit what and how we perceive. In slightly different words, "moral codes assume a particular view of the facts."[12] Moreover, seldom is a single view of human nature and human history maintained through different codes. For example, "the patriotic code assumes one kind of human nature, the commercial code another." A single person can, often does, behave differently in his several capacities as family man, employer, and political leader. The codes vary not only in the same person and among persons in the same social set; they differ yet more widely among social sets or between nations or races. As we know, peoples or nations having the same religions do go to war with each other.[13]

The codes exercise a subtle and pervasive influence on the formation of public opinion. That leads to one of Lippmann's broadest generalizations in the book: "The orthodox theory holds that a public opinion constitutes a moral judgment on a group of facts. The theory I am suggesting is that, in the present state of education, a public opinion is primarily a moralized and codified version of the facts. I am arguing that the pattern of stereotypes at the center of our codes largely determines what group of facts we shall see, and in what light we shall see them."[14]

The great variations in what contending factions in public affairs paint as factual are explained largely by what they set out to

[11] Ibid., pp. 117–118.

[12] Ibid., pp. 119–120, 123.

[13] Ibid., pp. 124–125.

[14] Ibid., p. 125. This is less than accurate of some of the previous discussions of the subject. See particularly James Bryce, *The American Commonwealth* (1888), vol. II, pt. IV, pp. 209–334.

see; they look upon their findings not as interpretations, but as
reality. Thus we see villains and conspiracies because it is easier
to explain failures or complex, perhaps only partially known circumstances as the work of agitators, spies, profiteers, or corrupt
politicians.

In the chapter on the detection of stereotypes there is again
much vivid writing, but little comfort for those who have faith in
popular government. In an earlier chapter the remark in one of
William James's letters, "No one sees further into a generalization
than his own knowledge of detail extends," was quoted. Here
Lippmann quotes James on what he called the "faith ladder" and
applies it to the stereotype fiction of the labor movement, in which
"an idealized mass moves towards an ideal goal."[15] The truth, as
Lippmann sees it, is that, because our love for the absolute is so
great, we generally see only sharp dichotomy—on the one hand,
unrelenting evil, on the other, unadulterated good. The influence
of his recent experience at Paris is evident: "It is not enough to
say that our side is more right than the enemy's. . . . One must insist that our victory will end war forever, and make the world
safe for democracy. . . . Real space, real time, real numbers, real
connections, real weights are lost. The perspective and the background and the dimensions of action are clipped and frozen in the
stereotype."[16]

The two chapters in Part IV, "Interests," are nearer to Madison's well-known, though very brief and often misinterpreted discussion, in the tenth *Federalist*, of the causes of faction than to
orthodox socialist theory. With Madison, Lippmann agrees that
men will be divided by their relation to property, as well as by
religious or political opinions or by attachment to leaders. But
Madison is noting the causal relationship, not between property
and opinions, but between differences of property and differences of opinion. "You can tentatively infer a probable difference
of opinions," Lippmann writes, "but you cannot infer what those

[15] Lippmann, *Public Opinion*, p. 152 (the reference is to William James,
Some Problems of Philosophy, p. 224).
[16] Lippmann, *Public Opinion*, p. 156.

opinions will necessarily be." And even after Marx and Lenin, we have no clear light on mankind's social behavior, because economic position is but one factor in determining public opinion. The truth is that "the socialist theory of human nature is . . . an example of false determinism."[17] Men ordinarily, perhaps always, pursue their interests. But how they will interpret and how they will pursue them are not determined. In the defects of determinism Lippmann finds a basis for a kind of optimism, though one shrouded in rhetoric, not delineated beyond the generalization that there is more to the future than we know, but we can choose our own standards of what is good and need not give up hope or slacken our effort.

Part V returns to earth with the title, "The Making of a Common Will." The problem is how a common will or purpose emerges from individual ideas or purposes. How, according to democratic theory, do so many people, each with his own very strong private feelings, ever come together in a common purpose. He mentions Le Bon and quotes Sir Robert Peel on "that great compound of folly, weakness, prejudice, wrong feeling, right feeling, obstinacy and newspaper paragraphs which is called public feeling." Others, concluding that definite aims somehow do emerge from drift and confusion, explain it by invoking "a collective soul, a national mind, a spirit of the age which imposes order upon random opinion."[18]

Lippmann thinks that we need not resort to the mysticism of the oversoul, and he takes as an example the speech Charles Evans Hughes made in 1916 to bind together the Republican party shattered in 1912. It is a fairly typical example of how a public opinion—or at least a surface unity—can be constituted out of divergent elements by the use of vague phrases and symbols that mean different things to persons who can agree only on generalizations that do not induce friction about specifics. Similarly, the Fourteen Points was long on emotion and general promises of

[17] Ibid., pp. 182, 185, 187.
[18] Ibid., pp. 193, 197.

a bright future, but vague on precisely what was involved or how it could be achieved.

The use of generalizations and symbols in the First World War, so vivid to Lippmann when he wrote *Public Opinion*, seems today less pertinent than the integration of sentiment in the decade before 1789, which made possible a nation where before there had been localism bounded, at the most, by colony or state lines. He gives too great a part in that remarkable change of opinion to Hamilton, a native of the West Indies and therefore not fiercely loyal to one state, and too little to many men who were ardently attached to a state but transcended their state loyalties. Among those he does not mention are Washington, Franklin, Madison, Adams, Marshall, James Wilson, Gouverneur and Robert Morris, scores of less well known Federalists, and some who became Antifederalists, though they supported union in 1787–1788.[19]

Mass action is rarely possible without some sort of leadership or organization. The leaders formulate the proposals; the action of the mass is limited to saying yes or no. The leaders know the value, the necessity, of employing symbols and exploiting loyalties. They know that it is easier to deal with, perhaps to investigate or even punish purported malefactors than to work out a policy that comes to terms with the essential factors in the equation. Often this leadership alleges that a program being advocated simply embodies what then exists in the public mind. This attempt is usually erroneous and misleading, for "thought is the function of an organism, and a mass is not an organism." The fact is that "the manufacture of consent" is a more highly developed art than ever before; it is an old art brought to new heights in recent years.[20] Lippmann's former hero, Theodore Roosevelt, was no amateur at this art.

Part VI borrows its title from Alexis de Tocqueville, who, in *Democracy in America*, wrote: "I confess that in America I saw more than America; I sought the image of democracy itself."

19 Ibid., pp. 217–219.
20 Ibid., pp. 243, 248.

Lippmann begins this discussion of the image of democracy by lamenting the dearth of books on public opinion, supposedly the basic factor in democracies. Compared to the mass of material on that subject today, some of it certainly stimulated by Lippmann's work, there was very little in 1922, but he would have found Bryce and, for that matter, Tocqueville more valuable than the few writings he does mention. His statement that "democracies . . . have made a mystery out of public opinion," as other theories have out of fate or the divine right of kings, is only partly correct. It suits Lippmann's thesis to find that the founders of popular government acted on the premise that the art of governing was naturally endowed. The concept of self-centered man, upon which all political theory from Plato and Aristotle through the democratic theorists was based, held that man saw "the whole world by means of a few pictures in his head."[21] This is, of course, inexcusable as a capsule history of political theory. It is true enough that the range of problems or issues with which the self-contained citizen should have an informed opinion is far more extensive than it was two hundred or two thousand years ago, but then the means of communication and information have correspondingly improved.

In the formative period of the United States, the accepted theory was that of the omnicompetent citizen who was interested in public affairs and capable of dealing with them. This view, which Lippmann attributes particularly to Jefferson, is based upon a nation of self-contained communities with its codes of morals, its standards of behavior and of reaction to facts all accepted.

A chapter somewhat misleadingly entitled "The Role of Force, Patronage, and Privilege" begins with the assumption that the men of the Federal Convention saw their problem as "to restore government as against democracy."[22] What Lippmann means, or should mean, is that they sought a stronger and more effective

[21] Ibid., pp. 254, 262.
[22] Ibid., p. 278.

union. Democracy, a term then used only to describe direct, as opposed to representative, government in towns or city states, was not interfered with. Popular power was carried further than in any national government covering so large an area. Nor is it helpful to say that the Federalists saw the doctrine of checks and balances as the remedy for the problem of public opinion. Everyone today knows that the Antifederalists argued that the amount or kind of separation of powers in the proposed constitution was an inadequate protection to the liberty almost everyone—except Hamilton—wanted. They were not seeking to "neutralize" public opinion, though it is perfectly clear that they distrusted the kind of simple majority rule that Tom Paine saw as the solution of all problems. To Jefferson, Lippmann gives the chief credit for changing a conservative Federalist system into something that had not been intended. This is not the place to point out all the flaws in Lippmann's J. Allen Smith–Charles Beard version of the age of the founders, but surely it is evident that Jefferson's election did not change the system—which as a system Jefferson highly approved—from an oligarchy to a democracy.[23]

One of the chief means of bringing about the change, indeed, one of the very few specified, was patronage. Lippmann attributes the idea to Jefferson, though both Washington and Adams followed it and though there were few partisan removals in Jefferson's term. Of course, though this is not pointed out, one of the shrewdest actions by that remarkable politician was the incorporation of most of the Federalist program (with the notable exception of the Alien and Sedition laws and the lameduck Judiciary Act of 1801) into the policies of the new party. Well before Jackson became president and began to justify patronage on partisan, and democratic, grounds, the Federalist party had ceased to exist. What Jackson did, it appears, was to found a new governing class, with rotation in office among its members, the consequent building of political machines, and the loss of prestige of representative government. Localism has continued, but patronage and

[23] Ibid., pp. 276–284.

pork have been powerful instruments in binding the leaders and the localities into something like union. To this there are only two alternatives, "government by terror and obedience" (this is "in decay"—Stalin and Hitler were unknown in 1922) and "government based on such a highly developed system of information, analysis, and self-consciousness that 'the knowledge of national circumstances and reasons of state' is evident to all men." The latter is just beginning to develop, so that we must, apparently like Hamilton, one of the "great state-builders," continue to rely upon patronage and privilege.[24]

A chapter on a now almost forgotten body of theory, guild socialism, may be passed by. It is followed by a five-page chapter, "A New Image." Here Lippmann asserts that the fallacy of democratic theory lies in its concentration on the source, not the exercise of power, in the assumption that power properly derived would, inevitably, produce good results. What is important is the expression of the people's will. Of course, the dignity of man thus rests uncertainly on the shaky assumption that the citizen will in the course of nature demand good government and just laws. Whether this is indeed the whole of the assumption underlying the theory of democracy, even as Lippmann saw it in his first two books, is highly doubtful, but it is his theory in 1922. When, he says, voters do not vote for laws that promote "a minimum of health, of education, of freedom, of pleasures, of beauty," democratic theory looks silly.[25]

It is unlikely that, in the foreseeable future, men will see the invisible environment with such startling clarity that public opinion on all matters of government will immediately and naturally become sound. Some method must be found of developing greater numbers of men whose expertise can keep the pictures of the invisible world objective. Somehow we must work out standards and audits that will enable the general public to know whether

[24] Ibid., pp. 291–292. Lippmann's view of Hamilton, like his contrasting view of Jefferson, seems to owe more to Croly than to the factual history of their ideas and achievements.

[25] Ibid., pp. 312–313.

there are information, standards, and controls that make up for the deficiencies in the range and the interest of the self-centered individual.[26]

In Part VII Lippmann is dealing with a subject of which he had a great deal of immediate experience, newspapers. The assumption underlying almost the whole of his book is found on every page of that section, certainly on its first page (317) and its last (365). In between comes a brilliant and very readable analysis of the failings of newspapers as instruments to provide the information, the knowledge, the truth about the world that the democrat, the defender of freedom of speech and the press—from John Milton to Zechariah Chafee—assumes to be the basis for self-government.

Political scientists and political philosophers from the time of Aristotle to the recent founders of modern democratic theory have had little to say about the way in which men would get the essential information on which the will of the people was to be based. They have assumed that, given freedom of inquiry and expression, the truth would prevail. Lippmann does not question the value of civil liberties; he does assert that these freedoms do not guarantee sound public opinion. In particular, adequate attention has not been given to newspapers in connection with the formation of opinion. Yet they are singularly inadequate. Newspapers are not to be compared with the public schools or the churches, nor journalism with the legal, medical, or technical professions. The consumer pays for what he gets from these institutions or professions, whereas newspapers are practically free. Advertising bears most of the cost, though advertisers do not exert as much influence on the standards and completeness of accurate coverage by newspapers as does the taste of the buying public. The public wants to be entertained, excited, provided not with full details of what is essential to a true picture of the complexities of the world outside, but with the stories or features that interest it. The accuracy of a story is rarely tested; a reader cannot take to court a news-

[26] Ibid., pp. 310–314.

paper he thinks has misled him. The newspaper stakes its life on the loyalty of its buying public. That public can judge the reliability of reporting only where it has personal, therefore local, experience.[27]

When *Public Opinion* was written, Upton Sinclair's *Brass Check*, an attack on the absence of impartiality in the capitalist press, was a subject of recent interest and discussion. The point is well made that not even Upton Sinclair finds the noncapitalist or radical press "a model of truthfulness and competence."[28] The real problem is not who owns the newspapers but what the nature of news is.

Newspapers do not, could not, keep an eye on everyone or on all events. The news does not reflect social conditions, but reports an unusual or spectacular event. News and the truth are not the same, for the truth, the whole truth, is far more than what is judged to be news. News is, on the whole, the exceptional. Both Mr. Sinclair and his opponents assume that the words *news* and *truth* are interchangeable; this is far from correct. Whereas "the function of news is to signalize an event, the function of truth is to bring to light the hidden facts, to set them into relation with each other, and make a picture of reality on which men can act."[29] What Lippmann had previously pointed out about the lack of interest of the buying public only adds emphasis to this distinction between news and the kind of full information few newspaper buyers would read even if the press published it.

It is not the function of the journalist or the press to report the social facts, the broad knowledge required by the democratic theory of public opinion. The defects in the formulation of policy lie deeper than the shortcomings of the press, whether capitalist or radical. Men "cannot govern society by episodes, incidents, and eruptions." The remedy is "in social organization based on a system of analysis and record ... in the abandonment of the theory of

[27] Ibid., pp. 317–329.
[28] Ibid., pp. 336–337.
[29] Ibid., p. 358.

the omnicompetent citizen, in the decentralization of decision, in the coordination of decision by comparable record and analysis."[30]

The failure of self-governing peoples to transcend their casual experience and their prejudices cannot be overcome by improvement of newspapers, for newspapers do not and cannot be expected to provide an accurate picture of the world. Without that accurate picture, not only governments, but also "schools, newspapers, and churches make . . . small headway against the more obvious failings of democracy, against violent prejudice, apathy, preference for the curious and the trivial as against the dull important." Lippmann concludes his section on newspapers with the sentence, "This is the primary defect of popular government." That is a sweeping generalization, but it is followed by the statement that "all its other defects can, I believe, be traced to this one."[31] It would appear that he has come to the conclusion that satisfactory, intelligently directed popular government is simply and finally impossible, that the prejudices, apathy, and desire for excitement and trivial entertainment destroy the very premises on which the theory was founded. But, having devastatingly analyzed, as few Americans since the time of Alexander Hamilton, Fisher Ames, and John Randolph of Roanoke had done, the failings of the entire concept of government based upon the will of the people, Lippmann proposed a remedy. Part VIII is given the hopeful title, "Organized Intelligence."

All complex societies have looked for help to men of special wisdom, to "augurs, priests, elders." Even American democracy, with its faith in the omnicompetent citizen, entrusted the management of government to lawyers. Legal assistance of the traditional kind, however, is inadequate to cope with the enormous growth and the rapid changes technology has brought to the Great Society. If it is to be governed, men must gain understanding of its nature and its complex variations, and this will require the work of specialists in social science, just as its creation required the ef-

---

[30] Ibid., p. 364.
[31] Ibid., p. 365.

forts of engineers, chemists, geologists, and physicists. The specialist in gathering and organizing information about this vastly intricate society in which we live is as essential to government as the scientist or the technologist is to industry. True, democratic theory has lagged behind democratic practice. There are many organizations that employ research for the benefit of almost all units of government. They are a good beginning, but no more. They do not adequately overcome the difficulty of dealing with an unseen reality. It is essential that we have intelligence bureaus that will have as their function the securing and organizing of the information on which alone a true body of public opinion and social opinions can be based. The present instruments of analysis are crude, vague, and inadequate. But we know that environments can be reported accurately and in a way to overcome prejudice and subjectivism.[32]

There is no electoral device that will do this: "You cannot take more political wisdom out of human beings than there is in them." (Lippmann's remark is almost the same as the one made by the classic of nineteenth-century democratic theory, John Stuart Mill's *Representative Government*.) Nor will any alteration in the system of property strike at the heart of the problem.[33]

Lippmann appears to have abandoned the possibility of democracy, of government based upon the knowing and active consent of the governed, only to come to the rescue with a solution that would require a combination of indefatigable research and analysis and the willingness of men to make use of the results of such investigations.

Chapter XXVII, "The Appeal to the Public," is primarily an argument that the citizen cannot be expected to have expert opinions on all questions, and that the burden of investigation, of analysis, of all but the final decision should therefore be the func-

---

[32] Ibid., pp. 369–397.

[33] Ibid., p. 397. Mill's sentence is: "In politics, as in mechanics, the power which is to keep the engine going must be sought for outside the machinery" (*Representative Government*, ch. I, p. 244 of the Everyman edition of *Utilitarianism, On Liberty, Representative Government*).

tion of the responsible administrators. These experts are presumably almost as selfless, as dedicated only to the welfare of the
state and community, as Plato's guardians. Lippmann concedes
that nearly all of us, except those particularly concerned about
one or another issue or policy, do not have the time, the attention,
or the interest to deal with most public affairs. "The outsider," and
that term applies to most of us nearly all the time, can be expected
to do little more than arrive at decisions after the event and judge
the basis of the propriety of the procedure followed. The general
public cannot be expected to deal with the substance of intricate
matters, with the infinite complexity of questions up for decision.
The average citizen is likely, if this burden is placed on him, to
come up with little beyond "some soul-filling idea like Justice, Welfare, Americanism, or Socialism."[34] It is precisely these substitutes
for knowledge and understanding of the real issue involved that
we must avoid. Prejudice, stereotypes, vague emotions, and en-
thusiasms are sorry substitutes for the truth.

All this is delightful and evocative of utopias from Plato to Edward Bellamy. How, given everything Lippmann has written in
the preceding pages of his book, can we expect the citizen to
abandon all his limitations of time and attention, of stereotypes
and interests, of localism and privilege, of affection for the sensa-
tional rather than for the stern truth? We are not told, except in
the vaguest terms, and those nearer to what ought or must be done
than the kind of analytical terms used when the author is under-
mining what he assumes to be the accepted theory of public
opinion.

Chapter XXVII, "The Appeal to the Public," is a brief one. The
final chapter, "The Appeal to Reason," is even shorter. In its seven
pages what we have is not so much a rational discussion of an exceedingly difficult problem of the theory of government based on
the consent of the governed as it is a resort to a strange combination of humility and emotion. Lippmann begins by saying that he
has written and thrown away "several endings to this book." Then

[34] Lippmann, *Public Opinion*, pp. 400–402.

he points to the example of Plato, who confesses that his ideal will never exist until "philosophers are kings, or the kings and princes of this world have the spirit and power of philosophy." He might have added that Plato agreed that his picture of the perfect society was to be found in heaven, for on earth it nowhere exists. Lippmann does say that, having made his admission, Plato "picked up the tools of reason, and disappeared into the Academy, leaving the world to Machiavelli."[35] "The Appeal to Reason" is more nearly an appeal to hope and emotion. There are a few sentences where the analysis of the limitations of the public is recalled, as when, invoking Plato's allegory of the ship and the true pilot, he agrees that the pilot who knows his job is difficult to identify, and that most of his crew will not be convinced.

There are many reasons why politics cannot yet dispense with a kind of intelligence, strength, and belief neither grounded in nor governed by reason, for there are too many facts too undifferentiated for reason to comprehend. Among those reasons is the state of social science. Its methods are so imperfect that in many of the serious decisions and most of the casual ones there is yet no adequate basis for a rational choice. How and where do we get the experts who are to make the investigations? We are not told, yet surely this is, as it has always been, one of the essential and most difficult questions in political theory. And Lippmann appears to throw in the towel when, on the next to the last page of the book, he ends a paragraph with this sentence: "The number of human problems on which reason is prepared to dictate is small."[36]

The final page is clearly a rhetorical flight from the relatively cool analysis found in all except the last two chapters. The references are not to Plato but to the horrors and follies of the World War and the Versailles peace conference. "Great as was the horror, it was not universal. . . . if amidst all the evils of this decade you have not seen men and women, known moments that you would like to multiply, the Lord himself cannot help you."[37]

[35] Ibid., pp. 411, 412.
[36] Ibid., pp. 416–417.
[37] Ibid., p. 418.

The Phantom Public

Of the nine books by Lippmann here discussed, the sequel to *Public Opinion* is the easiest to summarize without doing injustice to its argument. *The Phantom Public* is not only a sequel; it is also a frank acknowledgment that, though Lippmann stands by his dissection of the shortcomings of what he believes to be the accepted assumption of the role of public opinion in democratic theory and by his analysis of the gross defects in that assumption and that theory, his proposal for remedying that state of affairs was sadly inadequate. In the present book the dissection depends more on similes and metaphors than did the analysis in *Public Opinion*, but the proposal for reform, if that is the appropriate word, is even less plausible. It is more dryly rationalistic than any ever proposed by the founders of representative democracy, whether the Utilitarians, Jefferson, or Madison.

On the opening curtain in *Public Opinion* was the figure of the prisoners chained in the cave from Plato's *Republic*. In *The Phantom Public* the place of honor is given to a quotation from that remarkable plea by Alexander Hamilton on June 18, 1787, that the new constitution to be proposed by the Federal Convention have a president and a senate elected for life, the former to have an absolute veto over Congress, the states to be mere administrative units of the national government—a plea listened to by the Convention and ignored by everyone. The sentence Lippmann quotes is: "The Voice of the People has been said to be the voice of God: and however generally this maxim has been quoted and believed, it is not true in fact."

Lippmann—unlike Hamilton, who spoke confidentially or wrote to friends of his preference for the British constitutional monarchy and hereditary House of Lords and very limited suffrage—does not explicitly oppose liberal democracy, though his support is highly qualified. Government has become too complex, too remote, too technical, too subtle to be controlled by the ill-

informed, confused, largely uninterested public that is supposed
to govern through something called public opinion. The citizen
has his own affairs and his own family to take care of. He lives in
a little circle of earning, spending, and personal problems, which
need have no particular relation to the multifarious and remote
issues with which government is concerned.

The various proposals for reforming democracy all take for
granted that the electorate has already attained, or is at least ap-
proaching, the competence to govern its own affairs. "I think it is
a false ideal. I do not mean an undesirable ideal. I mean an unattainable ideal, bad only in the sense that it is bad for a fat man
to try to be a ballet dancer.... The ideal of the omnicompetent,
sovereign citizen is, in my opinion, such a false ideal. It is unattainable. The pursuit of it is misleading. The failure to achieve
it has produced the current disenchantment."[38]

This statement leaves an insubstantial foundation for the theory
of democracy, at least for what Lippmann appears to think that
theory involves. Of course, it is not the theory of the tough-mind-
ed but hopeful men who founded our state and national systems
in 1776–1787, though it has some application to the dreamy vis-
ions of Rousseau (never influential in America) or to the simple
though eloquently stated ideas of Tom Paine.

In this book, as in *Public Opinion*, Lippmann repeatedly demol-
ishes the conception of the omnicompetent citizen. "The individual man does not have opinions on all public affairs." Who
thought he did have? "He does not know how to direct public
affairs." For what purpose do we have officers of government and
many thousands of full-time public employees whose responsibility is just that? "He does not know what is happening, why it is
happening, what ought to happen." There we come to an issue
deserving more careful analysis than the author gives to it. The
difference between the idea expressed in the sentence last quoted
and the two previous ones is a clue to Lippmann's confusion, but
he does not see it, for he goes on, as if there were no break in his

[38] Walter Lippmann, *The Phantom Public*, pp. 38, 39.

assumptions concerning the nature of democracy, to find no reason for assuming with some "mystical democrats" that the combined "ignorances in masses of people can result in wise government."[39] Who are these mystical democrats? Surely not George
Mason, John Adams, or James Madison, none of whom is mentioned, yet they are the chief authors of the most influential state
constitutions of the Revolution and of the national Constitution.

Government, in the years between elections, goes on as politicians, men in office, and other powerful men compromise and
reach decisions among themselves. Only occasionally will the
people be able to see and judge, much less affect, the nature of
these settlements. Public opinion cannot influence in any active
and continuing way so many complex and obscure matters. The
fact-finding agencies, which were to be saviors of public opinion
in the preceding book, are almost casually dismissed as giving no
more than an incidental assistance to the general public: "Their
findings are too intricate for the casual reader. . . . too uninterest-
ing."[40] So much for the remedy proposed in *Public Opinion*.

Nor can we see elections, which replace one group of men with
another, as an expression of the popular will. We vote for a candidate, but we choose neither who will run nor what his platform
and policies will be. It was a nineteenth-century commonplace
"that there was a deep wisdom in majorities which was the voice
of God." With Alexander Hamilton, Lippmann finds this unfound-
ed in fact. He does not go on to favor the highly centralized life-
term, strong, and, it is hoped, wise rule advocated by the young
Hamilton. Always, so he tells us from time to time in nearly all
his books, a liberal democrat, Lippmann is torn between his conclusions of the errors of the mystical democrats and his findings
of the failings in their view of government of and by the people.
The public does not really make its opinions known; it simply
lines up for or against a suggested course of action. The people do
not govern; they only support or oppose the individuals who
actually govern. The public cannot know about events from the

[39] Ibid., p. 39.
[40] Ibid., pp. 41–42.

inside out, cannot look at events and judge in the same way as those who know and who govern. The public "is inexpert in its curiosity, intermittent, . . . it discerns only gross distinctions, is slow to be aroused and quickly diverted . . . it personalizes whatever it considers, and is interested only when events have been melodramatized as a conflict."[41]

The traditional concept of the public as a check on its governors is less than adequate. Lippmann adds to the effectiveness of his denunciation of an unattainable idea with a vivid simile, not altogether unlike Plato's allegory of the cave. "The public will arrive in the middle of the third act and will leave before the last curtain, having stayed just long enough perhaps to decide who is the hero and who the villain of the piece. Yet usually that judgment will necessarily be made apart from the intrinsic merits, on the basis of a sample of behavior, an aspect of a situation, by very rough external evidence."[42] The possibility that the belated and hurried theater-goer will have a strong economic, religious, philosophical, or merely personal interest in the plot, the actors, and the outcome of the play, and will somehow manage to learn more than his passing glimpse of it on the stage, is not suggested. Yet there one finds an essential aspect of the theory of popular government.

Public opinion is clearly not a creative force. It can do no more than come down on one side or the other; "by holding the aggressive party in check, it may liberate intelligence. Public opinion in its highest ideal will defend those who are prepared to act on their reason against the interrupting force of those who merely assert their will."[43] That seems a very high ideal indeed, one almost impossible of attainment in the complexities of modern mass society, yet it is Lippmann's solution in this volume, as its later chapters make clear.

The argument is that public opinion cannot govern; it is unable to master the intricate issues and problems of society, and the

[41] Ibid., pp. 41–42, 58–64, 65.
[42] Ibid., p. 65.
[43] Ibid., p. 69.

"theory of democracy has not recognized this truth because it has identified the functioning of government with the will of the people. This is a fiction."[44] It is also not the traditional theory of constitutional, representative democracy in America, though the author is correct in his belief that some mystics and simplifiers have so conceived it.

The "public which directs the course of events.... is a mere phantom. It is an abstraction.... The public is not, as I see it, a fixed body of individuals. It is merely those persons who are interested in an affair and can affect it only by supporting or opposing the actors."[45] Aristotle's answer to this was to keep the community small and simple. This was, of course, the accepted Greek view of the city-state in an age of small farms and handcraft industry—and before Aristotle's one-time student Alexander the Great temporarily built his empire on conquest. Certainly that answer of Aristotle has limited application to the relatively huge and complex society of today, though other parts of the *Politics* are still legal tender.

It is unnecessary to follow Lippmann's somewhat repetitious belaboring of the proposition that the public is uninformed, generally uninterested, and that public opinion does not actively govern the affairs of the great society. What the public is (or should be) interested in is "not in the rules and contracts and customs themselves but in the maintenance of a regime of rule, contract and custom ... in the method of law, not ... the substance." The citizen cannot decide arguments on their merits. But though free and open debate may not give up any answers or even illuminate the problem very much, it does allow the debaters to expose each other, and so tends to locate and identify the bases of partisanship. And if the partisans are clearly identified, "debate will have served its main purpose."[46]

That full and open debate on public issues, as Jefferson and Mill and many others have asserted, is essential in a free society,

[44] Ibid., p. 71.
[45] Ibid., p. 77.
[46] Ibid., pp. 105, 114.

seems scarcely arguable. That it does not contribute anything to an understanding of the substance of the issues debated, as well as to the willingness of the contestants to abide by the rules of the game, is doubtful. It is more than doubtful that the public, which has most of the limitations Lippmann so skillfully and graphically set forth in both *Public Opinion* and *The Phantom Public*, will be content to consider only which contestant has more closely observed the rules of procedure. The tests proposed in this second attempt to provide a solution to the democratic dilemma are singularly unreal and abstract. The public is almost always far more interested in personages, personalities, and in slogans—sometimes oversimplified, perhaps misleading versions of the issues themselves—than in strict observance of rules of procedure. Lippmann offers no illuminating examples to make clear how his proposed tests would work, especially when emotions are involved, when feelings rather than rational analysis reign, when rival demagogues are seeking public support.

In this second book on public opinion, Lippmann does point out very convincingly many of the limitations of what he assumes to be the classical theory of the role of public opinion. He never stops to point out just who and how many of the founders of constitutional democracy as it is known in the United States, Great Britain, several of its Dominions, and a half-dozen or so countries of Western Europe hold the views he attributes to them. Neither Rousseau nor Tom Paine was, in fact, such a founder. The central theory of our kind of democracy (with more or less temporary and usually localized extravagances about the referendum and recall, particularly in the decades before Lippmann wrote) is that of electing officials to govern for us. Lippmann is not writing about Madison and Jefferson and Jackson and, except for one great speech, Lincoln. He is somehow assuming that the movement for greater participation in government that began in the late nineteenth century and continued into the first two or three decades of this century is the standard version. Many aspects of this movement, sometimes abbreviated into the saying "the cure for the evils of democracy is more democracy," or even "we have never tried democracy in this country," were relevant to the low level of politics in that era, but they are not the doctrine of the founders.

We can agree that he did say many things about public opinion that political scientists, including those equipped with formidable collections of data about voters and voting and even more formidable mathematical methods, subsequently discovered for themselves. What he does not do is fit his findings into an improved theory of government by the active consent of the governed.

3. The State as Mediator

A Preface to Morals

The only hope Lippmann offered in *The Phantom Public* was procedural—observance of the rules of free and open discussion and disclosure, a regime of rule, contract, and custom. This is a thin diet to offer the troops who insist on being emotional, loyal or disloyal, selfish, full of whims and caprices, who, in other words, want their say in decisions that, as they see it, affect them, and who, conversely, often care little about the relatively abstract rules by which the great game of politics is played.

Four years after settling for this strangely abstract and rational conclusion, Lippmann published his *Preface to Morals*, one of the most popular and widely read of his books.[1] Written during the last years of Calvin Coolidge's tenure in the White House, it ap-

---

[1] Published by Macmillan in 1929, by 1935 it had been reprinted at least fourteen times. It later appeared as a paperback, also by Macmillan.

peared in May of 1929, a few months before the Great Depression. It is, as the title indicates, focused on moral philosophy and only incidentally touches on political theory. That incidental treatment of the subject to which he devoted so many books, essays, speeches, and columns is important for the purposes of this analysis, for it indicates that Lippmann had temporarily retreated from the deep pessimism about the possibilities of effective self-government in democracies, and had done so in a way that related to a widely held point of view in the years just before the economic crash.

For the old religions and the foundation they afford for morals, Lippmann has a detached respect, but he appears to believe they are for the devout. The simple theism of the centuries before the Enlightenment has ceased to be adequate for the man of reason. Men no longer believe unquestioningly in a just and omnipotent god and so must base their ethical decision on something other than divine revelation. A dogmatic morality is no longer acceptable; therefore, men "must live by the premise that whatever is righteous is inherently desirable because experience will demonstrate its desirability."[2] The religion of humanism does not have its Ten Commandments handed down from God to His agent on earth. The teachers of humanism have to rely on mundane experience, not on authority but on intelligence applied to the affairs of men. Having argued in the two books on public opinion that man is but indifferently rational and rarely disinterested, Lippmann, four years later, immediately before the depression with which President Hoover was saddled, builds an almost convincing argument on the idea that in disinterestedness and rational inquiry we can find answers that, though not founded on the rock of revelation, will be the best available guides to moral standards and human behavior. This "humanistic view rests on human psychology and an interpretation of human experience."[3]

The argument of the book cannot fairly and adequately be

[2] Walter Lippmann, *A Preface to Morals*, p. 137.
[3] Ibid., pp. 138–139, 143.

stated in a sentence or reflected in a few quotations, but some sentences, such as those at the end of Chapter IX, do give a reasonably accurate clue to the tone and spirit of the book: "I venture, at least, to suggest that the function of high religion is . . . a prophecy and an anticipation of what life is like when desire is in perfect harmony with reality. It announces the discovery that men can enter into the realm of the spirit when they have outgrown all childishness." Such a concept necessarily places emphasis, not on obedience, reward and punishment, but upon "the conversion, the education and the discipline of the human will."[4] With Spinoza, many times quoted or referred to in the book, Lippmann agrees that this way of salvation is hard, is seldom found, but that all things excellent are as difficult as they are rare. This, he says, is the only acceptable religion for modern men. Evidently he holds a much higher conception of the human will than of human capacities in dealing with the issues and the complexities of social and political organization and government.

For the view of moralists like Ruskin and William Morris who propose a system of natural liberty that assumes that each man pursues his own interest, he has little but scorn. This view assumes that each man knows his own interest, when in fact few know and fewer pursue their true interests. Such a completely free society is not an order at all; there is "no system of rights and duties" in it. The doctrine of laissez faire meant that the most intricate technology ever devised "was given over to the direction of a class of enterprising, acquisitive, uneducated, and undisciplined men." All the regulatory laws of the nineteenth century were needed to enforce order among men who were left freely pursuing their own self-interests. But this kind of reform not only assumes that capitalist magnates will persist in their wicked ways unless coerced into civilized and humane practices; it also presupposes that those who police them, the men with political power, will themselves exercise wisdom and disinterestedness. Essentially the same assumption must be made about socialism. A revolution,

[4] Ibid., pp. 193, 195.

like that in Russia, may purge great numbers of existing ills. But
after the revolution comes the necessity of administering the
system and, as under capitalism, the government of industry "depends upon the character of the administrators."[5] The early utopias never included this inevitable problem in their descriptions.

Hope for the governance of industry under capitalism lies in
the fact that the complexities of the system, the inability of its efficient control by democratic politicians, are compelling industrial
leaders to develop ways of policing themselves.[6] In the first six
to eight months of 1929 this seemed to many to be the answer to
the problems of the tremendous growth of corporate wealth and
power. Before long, it appeared to at least as many to be another
form of utopian wishful thinking.

In 1928 and early 1929, Lippmann asserted with confidence
that political thinking was "notably inferior in realism and in
pertinence to the economic thinking which now plays so important a part in the direction of industry."[7] President Hoover must
have agreed wholeheartedly with this dictum. In the time before
the Great Depression and before Hitler's rise to power in Germany, it did seem that fanaticism (Russia and Italy apart) was
to be found mainly in areas isolated from the centers of civilization. The complicated and confusing nature of modern society is
forcing us to recognize that temperance, reconciliation, and
tolerance are the best means of bringing the disparate elements
of that society into a harmoniously functioning whole. It does not
follow that modern governments are administered with the wisdom we would wish, or that they no longer ignore many things
that cry out for attention. It does mean that "they cannot afford
the luxury of prolonged disorder or of a general paralysis."[8]

The nature of government is undergoing fundamental change.
Ideas inherited from the past no longer apply. Modern politics
differs greatly from that of previous ages in one crucial way: the

[5] Ibid., pp. 247–248, 249, 250.
[6] Ibid., p. 255.
[7] Ibid., p. 260.
[8] Ibid., pp. 271, 273.

power to govern only rarely rests with one man who commands and is obeyed. "The power is distributed and qualified so that power is exerted not by command but by interaction."[9]

Since the first business of government is not to govern men's affairs, but to bring harmony among men directing their own affairs, Congress and the other agencies of government can do little more than reflect "the most stable compromises among the [many] interests." It follows that "what the government really does is not to rule men, but to add overwhelming force to men when they rule their affairs." If laws do not reflect the desires and interests of the public—as in the case of the prohibition amendment and laws—the laws go unenforced. The real authority of today does not rest with the state, but with the people.[10] There is, to be sure, a difference between the politician and the statesman—the former "stirs up a following," the latter "leads it." But it remains true that the chief task of statesmanship is to act as arbitrator, reconciler, to work for balance, for harmony—to give the people "not what they want but what they can learn to want." This demands "the insight which comes only from an objective and discerning knowledge of the facts, and a high and imperturbable disinterestedness."[11] One may ask where we are to find such Platonic guardians, what has become of the defects and dangers of public opinion, even whether this conception of statesmanship is consistent with the views advanced only a few pages back about the role of government as mediator among desires and interests.

In *Public Opinion* Lippmann wrote that Plato, having described his ideal society, then pointed out that on earth it nowhere exists, deserted the scene, and disappeared into the Academy, leaving the world to Machiavelli. In his *Preface to Morals* he sketches the outlines of a new political theory that is an uncertain combination of the state as neither strong nor decisively important and of the

9 Ibid., p. 275.
10 Ibid., pp. 277, 278–279.
11 Ibid., pp. 282–283.

need for high and disinterested statesmanship, but he does not follow Plato's example of saying that on earth such men are few and are rarely in high office. He simply stops the discussion of morals as applied to politics and turns the page to a chapter entitled "Love in the Great Society." The next and final chapter is "The Moralist in an Unbelieving World."

4.□ Security through a Compensated Economy

The Method of Freedom

Arthur Schlesinger, Jr., writes of *The Method of Freedom*, a revised version of the "remarkable Godkin Lectures of 1934," that it is "in some respects [the] most brilliant and prophetic" of Lippmann's works.[1] This assessment of the book is doubtless influenced by the fact that in it Lippmann writes sympathetically of President Franklin D. Roosevelt's New Deal, an attitude he was soon to reverse, even to the extent of supporting Governor Landon for the presidency in 1936;[2] in *The Good Society*, published in 1937, Lippmann finds the New Deal dangerously far on the road toward totalitarianism. As Professor Schlesinger points out, Lippmann

[1] Arthur Schlesinger, "Walter Lippmann: The Intellectual v. Politics," in the book of essays edited by Marquis Childs and James Reston, *Walter Lippmann and His Times*, p. 213.

[2] Childs and Reston (eds.), *Walter Lippmann and His Times*, p. 15.

had held widely varying views of Roosevelt from 1920 (high praise) to 1932 ("a pleasant man who, without any important qualifications for office, would very much like to be president") to 1933, when he saw the hundred days from March to June as a period in which "we became again an organized nation confident of our power to provide for our own security and to control our own destiny."[3]

Whether *The Method of Freedom* is or is not the most brilliant, or, what is a little different, most characteristic, or, still different, most important of his books on political theory is arguable. Certainly the editors of *The Essential Lippmann* thought it almost insignificant as a source of Lippmann's political theory. Whatever its rank among his books, it has not been one of the most widely read. Indeed, it may be the least well known. Except for *The New Imperative* (1935), it is the last of his books on political theory in which his views are in substantial harmony with the tendencies of the times in his country. In that respect it resembles most closely the two books of his youth, written two decades earlier. In another respect he has changed, at least from the somewhat diffident title of 1913, *A Preface to Politics*. Now we have *The Method of Freedom*. The change from *A Preface* to *The Method* characterizes all his later titles.

In the foreword to *The Method* Lippmann reverts to his general attitude of twenty years before to the extent of stating firmly that one devoted to the good life and to a regime of liberty must be prepared to change the means ("even the Gods on Olympus took diverse shapes") and to distinguish between the policies of free states in the nineteenth century and the essentials of free government in this era. Liberty can no longer mean precisely what it did during the preceding century. For today "the defense of liberty requires positive and affirmative convictions and principles." Almost everywhere liberty is on the defensive. A positive approach to the defense or method of liberty has appeared in the

[3] Schlesinger, "Intellectual v. Politics," in ibid., pp. 210–211. See also his *The Crisis of the Old Order*, pp. 96, 362, 395, 291, and *The Coming of the New Deal*, p. 22.

collective action followed in free nations with a highly developed capitalist economy. Lippmann makes no claim to have originated the "general principles which appear to me to have animated the measures which show the greatest promise of restoring and maintaining order in a regime of liberty.... My highest hope would be to be able to say, as Montesquieu did in *The Spirit of the Laws*: 'I have not drawn my principles from my prejudices but from the nature of things.' "[4]

When men's lives are carried on in a state of confusion, the old certainties tend to give way to revolutionary ideas and methods; the familiar ways of doing things no longer work. Although we are now living in an era of confusion, it does not follow that those in search of a political creed should be so credulous as to resort to Marx or Spengler. What is needed is not a philosophical treatise, however awesome the challenge of its new version of history, but rather an experimental method relying on close attention to the particular conditions of the present and the fullest exercise of what man can know of how best to govern. This, it appears surprisingly, is the method of Burke, of "the English speaking peoples [who] have wrought for themselves a not inglorious destiny and a not inconsiderable influence in the affairs of mankind."[5] Whether Burke, except in his attitude toward the American colonies and toward Ireland, is a happy choice to represent the English ability (since 1688) to adapt to changing circumstance without resorting to revolution or to dictatorship is dubious; it is clearer that the social doctrine of Coolidge and Mellon was anachronistic, a hearkening back to the days before the war, even before Roosevelt's and Wilson's reforms, to the nineteenth-century conservatism of Mark Hanna.[6]

The old conservatism no longer meets the needs, much less the desires, of the mass of people, because the private capitalism of the nineteenth century has become an anomaly. The First World War disrupted the system, led to managed, centralized national

[4] Walter Lippmann, *The Method of Freedom*, pp. vii–xi.
[5] Ibid., p. 7.
[6] Ibid., p. 8.

economies, and war systems affected the economies of peace. No
longer could average men absorbed in their own affairs make the
effort to manage them. By 1931 postwar reconstruction had col-
lapsed. Today people want security. After twenty years of war
and reconstruction, they now care less for abstract rights and
freedoms than for safety and private security. This passion for
peace and security takes shape as communism or fascism in some
countries, as the New Deal or some program of relief in others.[7]

Although the crisis meant the death of laissez faire, there are
numerous alternatives. For that matter, both Adam Smith and
John Stuart Mill recognized exceptions. And under the old capitalism there were many exceptions to free competition, among
them labor unions, high tariffs, trusts, mergers, combines, and
holding companies. What is new is that today the state is "com-
pelled to look upon the economy as a national establishment for
which it is responsible and not as a mere congeries of separate
interests which it serves, protects, and regulates. . . . the assumptions of laissez faire have given way to the assumptions of collectivism."[8] Even President Hoover, who had earlier celebrated
laissez faire and individualism along with other leaders of the
country, turned, when the bubble of prosperity burst, to collective
action. When he sought reelection in 1932, he did not campaign
on a laissez faire belief that the economy, let alone, would cure itself. Instead he recited proudly the long list of aids to banks, insurance companies, the prices of wheat and cotton, and the maintenance of wage rates. Hoover moved more slowly, with less luck
and fewer results, but "every major move made by Mr. Roosevelt
was in principle anticipated by Mr. Hoover."[9]

In the modern state it has become the responsibility of government to guard the economic security of its people. This is just as
much its function as protecting their independence. Indeed, a
modern government must be able to guarantee economic security
if it is to retain its independence and its position of power in the

[7] Ibid., pp. 10–14.
[8] Ibid., p. 28.
[9] Ibid., pp. 30–32.

world. Thus the great issues of today are not laissez faire versus collectivism, but "the kind of collectivism, how it is to be established, in whose interests, by whom it is to be controlled, and for what ends."[10]

There are two radically different kinds of collectivism. In Eastern Europe military collectivism has taken the form of communism and of fascism. In all these states there is dictatorship. There centralized decision has replaced distributed decisions. The governments are not limited by customs, contracts, constitutions, or ancient usages. Central planning and central control "has required censorship, espionage, and terrorism."[11]

The abandonment of the laissez faire, neutral state does not inevitably result in an absolute collectivism. In the free countries, especially those of the English-speaking peoples, experience and native genius have shaped a system of control neither laissez faire, communist, nor fascist. This Lippmann calls "the method of free collectivism." The essential principle, in addition to ensuring a wide range of freedom in private transactions, is to compensate for any resulting imbalance by public actions. The method was not developed to meet the needs of a militarized state, but as a conscientious attempt to remedy the ills of capitalism.[12]

The sharp break from the conception of the role of government expressed in *A Preface to Morals* is clear and sweeping. Less obvious, but quite as important, is the contrast between the assumptions about the competence and character both of voters and of officers of government found in *The Method of Freedom* and in the two works on public opinion and those evident in two final books, in the group on political theory. These contrasts will be more fully discussed later, but surely it is apparent that the optimism of *The Method* exceeds even that of *A Preface to Politics*, and it is so different from the two later books, including the one published three years after *The Method*, that we can only wonder at the mood of euphoria that carried Lippmann in 1934

10 Ibid., pp. 35, 37–38.
11 Ibid., pp. 38–45.
12 Ibid., pp. 45–46.

to believing, or assuming, that a free government could not only "prevent fraud," but also equalize the bargaining power of the consumer and the employer, regulate public utilities, enact factory laws and minimum wage laws, break up monopolies, discourage harmful enterprises, restrict speculation, repress a too rampant individualism in the use of property, insure the weak against the hazards of existence, and prevent the strong from accumulating excessive wealth and power.[13] Among other things that must be abolished is the freedom of corporate secrecy. Moreover, these negative restraints are not enough. "It has become necessary to create collective power, to mobilize collective resources, and to work out technical procedures by means of which the modern state can balance, equalize, neutralize, offset, correct the private judgments of masses of individuals. This is what I mean by a Compensated Economy and the method of Free Collectivism."[14]

Clearly, the objectives of a modern state that sets out to provide for its citizens a Compensated Economy through the method of Free Collectivism are far removed from the conceptions of Adam Smith and even of the limited socialism of John Stuart Mill's final years and his last edition of *Political Economy*. What Lippmann seeks to demonstrate is not the humanitarian need for this vastly enlarged role of government, for this he does not examine as he does the defects of the traditional assumptions about public opinion in the book of that title. What he is intent on asserting is the radical difference between the absolute collectivism of communism or of fascism, and free collectivism. In the latter the government is always prepared to restore the balance should free enterprise tilt the scale too far in one direction. Somehow the initiative remains in private hands. Governmental intervention is not intended to replace free enterprise, but to protect it against its own mistakes and abuses. Government intervenes by remedial action, not by decree or interdiction. The "ideal is to prevent ex-

13 Ibid., p. 47.
14 Ibid., pp. 50–51.

cess; its general principle is not to impose a social order conceived by officials but to maintain in a changing order, worked out by the initiative and energy of individuals, a golden mean."[15] Because of this historically new alternative—the compensatory method—it is no longer necessary to choose between collectivism and private initiative, between state socialism and what had flourished for a time as a crude social Darwinism, an exaggerated individualism well beyond the mild laissez faire of Bentham and Mill.

Since no doctrine of social organization is spontaneous and universal, since none, from feudalism to fascism and communism, does more than express the character of what the significant part of that society holds to be true, every social order is, in practice, made up of many principles, some in conflict with others.[16] In England and America the relatively planned economy of Russia is prevented by the "wide distribution of property," by the complexity of the industrial system, above all by the fact that "a planned economy is an economy of scarcity and works effectively only in a seller's market. . . . The existence of plenty is a condition of liberty and multiplies the individual choices. . . . the consumer is master of the situation" and the ideal of planning "has not yet come to terms with an economy of abundance."[17] The millions who were out of work when Lippmann wrote that the consumer was master of the situation would doubtless have been puzzled by the contrast between their individual helplessness and their alleged share in mastery, but Lippmann is not here concerned with that difficulty. He is intent upon the argument that the highly developed system of capitalism will not submit to the rigid, militarized controls of absolute collectivism (as Germany was doing under Hitler in the years this book was written and published). But, because some sort of collective control is needed, we should adopt the method of "compensatory actions." At this point he cites central banking and the regulations of international payments as examples of compensatory method in practice. With these and

15 Ibid., pp. 57, 59.
16 Ibid., pp. 60–61.
17 Ibid., pp. 66–68.

other examples of that method, it is clear to Lippmann that our knowledge and experience offer no better way of coping realistically with the problems of a capitalist economy than that of compensatory action. We can be confident that this new social discovery holds great promise. It is probable, though not quite certain, that Lippmann was influenced by the early writings of John Maynard Keynes and other economists who were, before 1933, writing about the multiplicative effect of government deficit spending.[18]

After finding that the compensatory principle has great promise as a means of attaining economic stability and possibly some improvement in the lot of the unemployed, or, as President Roosevelt much more emphatically referred to the less fortunate one-third of the nation, the "ill fed, ill housed, ill clothed," Lippmann comes in Part III of this book to the problem of Government in a Regime of Liberty. Here we face the formidable difficulty of conflict between the principle of government by the rule of the people, and the compensatory rule that government should not always follow what passes for public opinion. Often it should go "contrary to prevailing opinion in the economic world. . . . Will a democracy authorize the government, which is its creature, to do the very opposite of what the majority at any time most wishes to do?"[19] At the present time there appears to be less conflict than Lippmann, writing in 1933–1934, anticipated.

The authors of the Constitution had few illusions about democracy, as Lippmann uses the word. Nor does he point out that the United States under the Constitution of 1787 was the standard, even the ideal, of self-government for generations. He follows the old historical line (a product of the Populist-Progressive era) that the Constitution was intended to make the country safe from

[18] Ibid., pp. 69, 71. Lippmann and Keynes were in frequent communication with each other. See R. F. Harrod, *Life of John Maynard Keynes*, pp. 315 n., 445, 450, 505, 555–556. Keynes's major work was not published until 1936, but he expressed the views regarding what Lippmann calls the compensatory role of government much earlier, both in writing and in conversation. See also Lawrence R. Klein, *The Keynsian Revolution*, pp. 36, 47, 40.

[19] Lippmann, *Method of Freedom*, p. 74.

democracy. It was, he writes, the later generations who brought greater popularization and produced a form of government susceptible to prevailing opinion.[20] The result has been a government by pressure groups. This phenomenon was clearly present in the Revolution and the Federal Convention, as witness the intransigence of the three southernmost slave states on the slave trade, and, in 1784, the defeat of Jefferson's proposal to prohibit slavery in the Southwest as well as the Northwest territories. And certainly Hamilton's financial policies were those of the banking-merchant-shipping groups. But the despondency of the books on public opinion is clearly evident in such statements as the sweeping generalization that the democracy highly responsive to prevailing opinion as expressed by pressure groups will be unable to govern a nation either at war or at peace when successful government requires stepping in and changing the social order. In an absolute democracy a dictator can claim the loyalty of the people by promising to deliver them from their own misgovernment. I am not certain which democracies he has in mind, other than Italy and Germany. Certainly he is incorrect if he includes those countries of Western Europe in which constitutional democracy was firmly established before 1914, as it was not in Italy and Germany. He then goes on to the generalization that democracy as well as capitalism "has to be reconstructed. . . . Absolute democracy [not located by country—surely it never existed in the United States, or Great Britain, or Scandinavia, or even Switzerland] was tolerable when the state was neutral. . . . But when the state becomes active, the ways of democracy have either to be adapted to the new responsibility, or democracy itself will be overthrown."[21]

The next section has the heading, "Representative Democracy: The Return to First Principles." By this he appears to mean the return to a system in which the initiative is, to a much greater degree, in the executive, not monopolized by the legislature. It is a perversion and corruption of constitutional government, a

---

[20] Ibid., pp. 75–76.
[21] Ibid., pp. 78–79.

cause of its weakness, when the modern state is governed by "coalitions of delegates responding to local coalitions of self-regarding pressure groups." No state controlled by such groups would be able to regulate the economy or to direct a free collectivism.[22]

It is perfectly clear that Lippmann has profound distrust of legislative–pressure group government. Nothing is said here about President Roosevelt's strong executive leadership in 1933 or his control over Congress in that year. The recurring emphasis is on the instability of the economic order that is the product of these self-seeking interests, which invariably flourish where the fiscal initiative is in the legislature and can be discouraged only where the executive initiative in fiscal matters is preserved.[23] The government need not abolish or suppress these interests, but it must be able to manage them. This appears to be virtually impossible when a large portion of the electorate have, or think they have, little to lose. It is not perfectly clear whether Lippmann here has reference to the propertyless, as distinguished from the great combinations of wealth and economic power. The latter would seem to be both a major source of pressure groups, and those who have, in the author's words, almost everything to lose. Apparently it is the former, the poor, or debtors, or mortgagees, who think they have no stake in society and who, when organized (as in trade unions, farmers' groups, or loose groupings of the unemployed) make up a tightly knit minority more powerful than the confused majority. As examples of these compact minorities he cites Tammany Hall and, a little surprisingly, the Republican party in its dominant years when it had the pension system, the public lands, the federal patronage, and the porkbarrel, the tariff, the natural resources, and subsidies. The party had, he concedes, principles, but it was "held together by these payments and privileges."[24]

Representative government in its distorted form is usually held together by cooperation between the two extremes of the social

[22] Ibid., p. 83.
[23] Ibid., pp. 85–90.
[24] Ibid., pp. 92–94.

spectrum: "the proletariat and the plutocracy." Incidentally, this admixture is not far from the one that Aristotle calls polity and finds to be the best for most states. But Lippmann finds that the insecurity of the proletariat is the greatest threat to free government. He even quotes Aristotle on the stability of government founded on the middle class, but does not go on to analyze the whole of his discussion of the subject. Of course Aristotle strongly favored a foundation in the men of middling property. So did Jefferson. Aristotle and Jefferson sought the security that Lippmann believes proceeds from a regime in which most men possess some property and want to keep it. He is at this time more Jeffersonian than he thinks. The chief difference is that Jefferson lived and wrote in an agrarian society, when land, or small farms, meant security, independence, and stability, whereas Lippmann was writing in an age when the family farm was beginning to decline and he saw the danger in the propertyless and in great corporate properties. The main bastion of freedom was and is private property. Tyranny has come when most men lacked property; modern examples are found in Russia, Germany, and Italy. Liberty has been maintained in France, Scandinavia, and the English-speaking countries largely because of the wide distribution of property, where most men had a stake in society.[25]

By private property Lippmann means an income, or source of income, that results in a feeling of security. In order to attain this feeling we should strike first at proletarian insecurity, not at the plutocracy. To do the latter does not result in making the poor richer, and it may result in a sharp reaction. Only by attacking poverty do we go to the root of the matter. In frontier society, with land yet to be settled, the socially deprived have a chance to stake out their own claim in the future. The problem of today is not the same as that of fifty years earlier. Social insurance of various kinds in the more advanced industrial countries aids the very poor, the unemployed, the handicapped, the aged—but all these are insufficient and offer a subtle affront to human dignity.[26]

[25] Ibid., pp. 95–101, 102.
[26] Ibid., pp. 103–106.

Of course we know that in Scandinavia they helped to provide security and stability, whereas in England less generous aids did not result in political insecurity, and in Germany a relatively old and advanced system of social insurance and government aids did not prevent Hitler.

Lippmann would go beyond the several kinds of social insurance and government aids and establish the right to work among man's natural rights. The unfashionableness of natural rights should not obscure the importance of the right of man to a job. This will mean public works on a large scale, work on which any citizen may find employment when he needs it. There is no lack of projects; they are inexhaustible and socially productive. Much of what we have been hearing in the last few years about reconstructing cities and means of improving rural health are cited as examples. Even the Civilian Conservation Corps and the Civilian Works Administration, hastily improvised though they were, demonstrate the practicality of this proposal. Not lack of public funds but lack of public imagination stands in the way of projects that, to be sure, do not result in an immediate profit in the marketplace, but do improve the resources and equipment of the nation. Idleness and unemployment are the truly expensive conditions.[27]

Guaranteeing the right to work fits in with the method of compensated economy, because it requires collective action when there are unemployment and no opportunities to get jobs. It is essential to a free collectivism that it ensure at all times the opportunity to labor. This can correct the irresponsibility that plagues democracy, and ensure both political and economic freedom. We cannot go back to the neutral state. Laissez faire is now an impossibility. But there is a great gulf between compensated economy and the absolute collectivism or planned economy that would mean endless misery. Freedom, not central control or dictatorship, is essential if men are to slip the bonds of the past and progress toward greater enlightenment. All human activity can-

[27] Ibid., pp. 107–108.

not, of course, be free, but human liberty should extend as far as possible, and authority no more than necessary. To free men the first principle will continue to be that "the state is the servant and not the master of the people."[28]

The New Imperative

The New Imperative is a book in form only, for it consists of a brief introduction and two essays, all written in the late spring of 1935. Their combined length is fifty-two pages. There is, however, adequate reason for including it, or them, here. The little book states, even more emphatically, the principle of *The Method of Freedom*, that "government must henceforth hold itself consciously responsible for the maintenance of the standard of life prevailing among the people."[29] This is what Lippmann, both in the introduction and in the title of the second essay, calls "the new imperative," which is as essential as the older imperatives to keep the peace and preserve the nation's strength against attack.

Just as we differ about particular issues of foreign policy or the relative importance for the common defense of airplanes and naval vessels, or about how to organize and support the police and the judiciary, so we may differ about governmental policies regarding the maintenance of economic health and political institutions. The essential point is that it is the function of government to deal with all of them. The economic order can no longer maintain itself without governmental controls.[30] People in a democracy now expect government to help when capitalism fails to satisfy their expectations, and they will support leaders who promise to provide relief from the misfortunes of crisis or economic depression.

A "clear and unprejudiced view of this new imperative" is obscured by the tendency to look at political change in the light

[28] Ibid., pp. 110–114.
[29] Walter Lippmann, *The New Imperative*, p. 1.
[30] Ibid., p. 3.

of Central or East European revolutions. This is an error.[31] We
are not on what Lippmann calls the "Berlin-Moscow road," but
are developing a system of economic and social controls neither
laissez faire nor centrally planned and administered. We are not
on a highway whose end is either communism or fascism, but one
which is a means of proceeding toward strengthening the economy and preserving the American political tradition.

In the essay entitled "The Permanent New Deal," Lippmann
attempts to defend the proposition that Roosevelt's New Deal
differs only in minor ways from the policies of President Hoover.
Hoover's program not only involved assuming national responsibility for dealing with the major evils of the depression, but also
embodied "working principles," to curb deflation, to provide
government aid to supplement the lack of private credit and aid
to the destitute where there are insufficient state and local resources, to reduce the hours of labor while maintaining wages,
to peg farm prices and encourage farmers to curtail production, to
organize industry with a view to secure common policies in respect to wages, hours, prices, and capital investment.[32] In short,
the author of that simplistic little book, *American Individualism*,
published by the then secretary of commerce in 1922, followed a
program which in almost all respects was that of Franklin Roosevelt, whose Commonwealth Club Speech in September of 1932
was the clearest indication before his election of what the New
Deal would involve.

Read today, this 1935 attempt to find that there is no sharp
break between the two administrations seems an extraordinary
exercise in wishful, or perhaps only badly confused, thinking,
especially when one remembers that the author was in a position
to observe from a front seat the legislative and administrative
measures taking place in 1933–1935. Even the ill-fated and far
too ambitious National Industrial Recovery Act (NIRA) was
only a minor "substitution of legal for compassionate marriages in
the realm of private monopoly." The Securities and Exchange Act

[31] Ibid., pp. 6–7, citing *The Method of Freedom*.
[32] Ibid., pp. 11–12, 19.

and the TVA went beyond the Hoover policies, but the essential point is that the old policy of laissez faire was abandoned by Hoover and the new policies that include "the management of money and the use of the national credit will be the permanent functions of the American government."[33]

It is unnecessary to point out the defects in Lippmann's argument that the Roosevelt New Deal was little more than a continuation of the Hoover policies. Hoover's bitter attack on the Roosevelt program in *The Road to Freedom* (1934) and in many speeches and articles, all denunciations of the New Deal as a European planned existence, and Lippmann's support of Landon in 1936, followed by *The Good Society* in 1937, are more than adequate commentaries on this thesis.

The second essay carries the book's title. Delivered as a Phi Beta Kappa address at Harvard in June, 1935, it is chiefly notable for its flat renunciation of the traditional doctrine of free trade as adequate for the contemporary world. "The doctrine of laissez faire is open to the devastating criticism that it is preached by men who wish other men to practice it."[34] It is no longer possible to have no national social policy, when many are hungry in the midst of surplus, millions are unemployed or homeless, houses and farms are without occupants, and machinery is unused. Today even a laissez faire policy would require direction by the state. The unrestricted play of economic forces, long the ideal of economists, is no longer tolerable. Liberty can be secured only by the action of a wise and watchful government. The particular circumstances of the nineteenth century, when England was far ahead in exporting manufactures and the frontier was still open in America no longer exist.[35]

Now the question is not whether we shall have a conscious policy. The question today is what policy we shall have and how it is to be administered. We cannot retrace our steps. Unless we are willing to be engulfed by "an imperious state socialism," we must

[33] Ibid., pp. 26–29, 37.
[34] Ibid., p. 46.
[35] Ibid., pp. 47–48.

learn to govern this new capitalist democracy. Otherwise, it will
drift into dangerous waters. Moreover, and this point is especially
important in view of what Lippmann was to write in his two
later books, it can be governed without the loss of personal
liberties. The use of state authority to redress the calamities of
the economic cycle does not mean the doom of civilization. The
great problem of today is to "find a true balance between liberty
and authority," not in the society of the nineteenth century, but
in that of contemporary and future circumstances. There is no
escaping the necessity to direct the order of society. We must
learn how to preserve "the integrity of our civilization against
proletarianism and plutocracy and the fatal diseases of concentrated power and concentrated wealth." We must therefore learn
how to govern the state in order to preserve man's natural rights.
"The barbarians [presumably in Russia, Germany, and Italy] are
again at the gates." Our goal is to "make invincible on this continent a commonwealth that invites the souls of men."[36]

[36] Ibid., pp. 49–52.

5. The Free Market, Civility, and Natural Law

The Good Society

If *The Method of Freedom* and *The New Imperative* have been the least widely read of Lippmann's books, *The Good Society* has been one of the most popular. There are a few threads uniting the books, but the main thrust is quite disparate. In the 1934 and 1935 books the major point is a search for security and liberty through a compensated economy, or freedom grounded in economic security, including a natural right to work guaranteed by the state. In *The Good Society* (1937), he has apparently come to despair of recent and contemporary roads to security and, instead of saying that laissez faire is dead, he seeks to return to the true theory and practice of the free market of Adam Smith and to the rule of law, either that of Coke and the common law or that of the Supreme Court.

Obviously shocked by the terrible examples of dictatorship in

Stalin's Russia and Hitler's Germany and despairing of any
strength in the League of Nations, which conspicuously failed to
deal with the Japanese seizure of Manchuria, Lippmann finds
that the disorders of our times began to appear about 1870 and
that the revolutionary dictatorships of 1937 are the products.[1] His
generalizations in the book are not limited to the totalitarian
regimes of Europe or Asia, but usually apply to the very countries
he had seemed to think of almost as models in establishing compensated economies without loss of essential liberties in *The
Method of Freedom*.

Never one to shrink from sweeping generalizations, Lippmann
begins by saying that "throughout the world, in the name of progress, men who call themselves communists, socialists, fascists,
nationalists, progressives, and even liberals, are unanimous in
holding that government with its instruments of coercion must,
by commanding the people how they shall live, direct the course
of civilization and fix the shape of things to come."[2] Progressives
and liberals are thus lumped with communists, fascists, and nationalists as planners and molders. All have joined to bring an
end to what has for centuries been the central concern of political
thought—the search for a law that is above that of arbitrary power. The seekers have looked to the uses of custom, to the law of
reason, to natural law. This conception lay behind the violent
efforts to undo the union of church and state, to liberate individual conscience, the fruits of knowledge and the arts, and the
activities of the market place from ruthless oppression. For a
thousand years men have struggled to subject king to constitution,
to set up for men and groups of men unassailable rights that would
be proof against the power of rulers or the rich, against the whims
of majorities or mobs. Lippmann gives examples of the minute
regulation of life and economic activity from the time of the
pharaohs to the eighteenth century and then comes up to the

---

[1] See the introduction to the 1943 edition of Walter Lippmann, *The Good
Society*, p. x.
[2] Ibid., pp. 3–4.

present by saying that "what Colbert did under Louis XIV was precisely what General Johnson and Secretary Wallace did under President Roosevelt."[3] This is not only one of the most exaggerated and untrue statements in any of Lippmann's books, but also one strikingly in conflict with several statements in the two previous books. Incidentally, both the NIRA and the Agricultural Adjustment Act over which Johnson and Wallace presided were held unconstitutional in 1935 and 1936—before *The Good Society* appeared.

For the corporate form of economic organization and property tenure he has high praise, though he dislikes monopolies. But big-scale enterprise is a natural result of modern technology. And if there is danger of corporate collectivism, those evils are multiplied a thousandfold by state control or ownership.[4] The fact is that "our generation has misunderstood human experience. We have renounced the wisdom of the ages to embrace the errors the ages have discarded."[5] This sounds almost exactly like the recent and contemporary denunciation of the New Deal by former President Herbert Hoover and would come as a surprise to one who had known Lippmann only through his books. The gap between *The Method of Freedom* and *The New Imperative* and *The Good Society* seems far wider than two or three years. The latter, at times, reads very much like the praise of Social Darwinism by William Graham Sumner over a generation earlier, long before the young Lippmann was first a mild socialist and then an enthusiastic liberal-progressive. Now he has found his home in the profound truth that the human race can advance only by giving greater freedom to individuals. One can only wonder whether the right to eat and freedom from hunger—or from discrimination—are included in his dogma. At any rate, he uses the inclusive term when he asserts that our generation "has returned to the heresies of absolutism, authority, and the domination of men by men. . . .

[3] Ibid., pp. 5–6, 10.
[4] Ibid., p. 15.
[5] Ibid., p. 19.

the choice of Satan offering to sell men the kingdoms of their world for their immortal souls."[6] He seems almost to want to go back past the Age of Reason to the Age of Faith (in which there was less than liberty for all except a very few individuals). He writes that men live in a troubled world where both custom and tradition have lost their authority. The old certainties had been losing strength for centuries, but the catastrophe of the Great War finally shattered them, and much that had never been questioned now required urgent and sometimes vital decision.[7]

Governments are limited in capacity because of the limitation of men. We simply do not know enough to have a planned society. This applies in the age of Roosevelt as in that of Pericles. Neither the mathematical logicians nor the social scientists, much less men in public office, have the tools or the ability to govern such enormously complex activities effectively. He makes a singularly inaccurate forecast about military mobility. Just as the complexity of the interests to be regulated makes it next to impossible to direct them from above, so a war of movement is possible only when there are small bodies of troops to be directed. With the terrible trench warfare stalemate on the western front from 1914 to 1918 in mind, Lippmann believes that the problems of supply will be so great that mobility will disappear.[8] Written in 1937, this discussion remained in the 1943 reprinting, even after the blitzkriegs in Poland, the Low Countries, and France, Rommel's campaigns in North Africa, and the fast and massive conquests by Japan in the Pacific had shown the idea of "diminishing mobility" of military forces to be utterly untrue. It thus provides no support to his argument that the size and complexities of industry and government render effective control inflexible, if not impossible.

With increased direction from above comes uniformity of goals, the sad result of the authoritative principle in action. No mere chance determined that the cult of the state should be attended

[6] Ibid., p. 21.
[7] Ibid., p. 23.
[8] Ibid., pp. 35–36.

by a pervasive feeling of the imminent doom of modern civilization. Despair is deepened by the discovery that human affairs are unmanageable; the organization has become too intricate for effective control. What results is a multiplication of individual desires and resistances. This generation has lost its most valuable inheritance—the belief that power should be limited by the capacity of rulers and by the interests of the entire community. Too often it is a collection of vested interests that influence and direct popular hopes.[9]

It must be repeated that Lippmann lumps together Stalin's Russia, Hitler's Germany, and the apparently erring constitutional democracies of Western Europe, Great Britain, and the United States. Government planning, even in the "free collectivism" of the previously called liberal democracies with their compensatory economies is per se bad, closely akin to, if not the same as, the totalitarian regimes of Soviet Russia, Germany, and Italy. All, all, is heresy and a generation is doomed to "reaction. . . . a terrible ordeal before they find again the central truths they have forgotten."[10]

When dealing with *The Method of Freedom*, I suggested that Lippmann may have been influenced by J. M. Keynes's earlier writings and by his own correspondence and conversations with that English economist. In 1937 Keynes, who in 1936 had published his extremely influential *General Theory of Employment, Interest and Money*, is rejected, and his place taken by Adam Smith. The ideal is the free trade of England in the Gladstonian era, an era that was the fruit of some seventy-five years of European thinking about the ills of regulation, when freedom was the method and the goal, when men thought in terms of more and more liberty as the power of special rights and privileges waned. Unhappily this period of freedom from restraint did not last very long. The protectionist doctrine gained support long before free trade gave way, and even John Stuart Mill in his later years assumed that the beneficial goals of liberal philosophy had been

[9] Ibid., pp. 37–40.
[10] Ibid., p. 41.

attained and that further progress would be toward collectivism. Not until three quarters of a century later, however, did collectivism come to dominate human affairs.[11]

In 1884 Herbert Spencer, in *The Man versus the State*, had warned that "every additional state influence strengthens the tacit assumption that it is the duty of the state to deal with all evils and secure all benefits." The accuracy of Spencer's prophecy may have been questioned at the time, but now those forecasts of doom are justified. Though the evils Spencer foresaw are most evident in Russia, Italy, and Germany, everywhere the cult of the state is gaining, "the idea [of the state as savior] is incarnate."[12]

It is scarcely worthwhile over thirty years later to follow the discussion of Chapter V, "The Totalitarian Regimes." The reign of Hitler and Mussolini ended with their defeat in war. Russia under Stalin was not the same as the Russia of the present time, though to westerners it is still close enough to absolutism to classify it as very distinct from the liberal, if regulated, democracies of Western Europe and the United States. What is interesting, and significant for an understanding of Lippmann's point of view in 1937, is the identity he finds between the Soviet Planning Commission and the system for appropriating funds for public works in the United States.[13] Any planned economy requires that one man or group must make the decisions; the remainder are the ruled. Yet in 1934 and 1935 he had praised, had argued for the necessity of just such planning and spending.

Despite the fact that every instance of collectivism we know of came into being either to wage war or to prepare for war, there are those who believe that collectivism can be established to ensure peace and abundance. The planners, such as Lewis Mumford, Stuart Chase, and George Soule, must necessarily gamble on the emergence of benevolent despots. They therefore leave un-

[11] Ibid., pp. 44-46.

[12] Ibid., pp. 52, 53. The reference is to Spencer's *Man v. State*, p. 33. Later in *The Good Society* Lippmann was critical of Spencer's doctrines.

[13] Lippmann, *The Good Society*, p. 79.

planned the very foundation on which their dreams rest. No method can be proposed for choosing the "despot," since in a planned society the people can only bow to their rulers. Thus the choice of who is to plan must be left to what Lippmann calls "irrational chance."[14]

In Chapter VII, "Gradual Collectivism," Lippmann acknowledges that Great Britain and the United States have not been under the control of fanatics who put planning above everything, but he argues that even these countries have been slowly moving toward collectivism for three generations. (Three generations back from 1937 takes us to the middle of the nineteenth century, rather early for the kind of collectivism here discussed to have begun.) Now the most basic principle of the democratic system requires the ruler to be always responsible to public opinion, and the public must be free to change that opinion or democracy no longer exists. Yet such unimpeachable democrats as Charles A. Beard have, in the name of democratic well-being, advocated a planned and administered society for the United States.[15]

But instead of making distinctions where there are in fact genuine differences, Lippmann sweeps on to a denunciation of all government by planning and controlled propaganda. The gradual collectivist is evidently, though perhaps unknowingly, a Benedict Arnold who would subvert the faith of the fathers and lead us into a reign of pressure groups and newly created vested interests. The pressure groups he has in mind are those created by laws favoring any special interest. The law may be a protective tariff, a law giving bounties to farmers, or one supporting labor unions. The protected or favored interest will immediately become a pressure group with interests it will assiduously seek to protect, probably to enhance. The result is the constant pressure of interested groups contending for aid by the government. The gradual collectivist has to assume that there is in the sovereign power an ability to discriminate among the various groups seeking aid

---

[14] Ibid., pp. 91, 105.
[15] Ibid., pp. 107–109.

and support. Madison's reasoning in the tenth *Federalist* is apparently irrelevant. Lippmann believes that the rule of law requires the government to act in accordance with a higher law, according to which such competing designs and desires are judged and decisions reached. In a democracy there is a continual creation of new special privileges, for the system of gradual collectivism not only protects rights already in existence but also acts to create new ones. Every group has been schooled in the idea that the state has not only the capacity but also a duty to make them wealthier. We have, as a result, a constant invitation to everyone to think in terms of greater and greater benefits, a collective mind attuned to ever-rising expectations. Not labor, but the government, is the cause of the belief in miracles. If some are benefited by public privileges or grants, why not others? Why not all? As a result, the people's productivity dwindles while their expectations soar. Thus the advance of gradual collectivism has become, throughout the world, a competitive struggle for privileges and power.[16]

Chapter VIII, "The Wars of a Collectivist World," read thirty-five years later, seems to be a curious combination of good and bad history, good and bad prophecy. The comparatively peaceful state of Europe between 1815 and 1914 Lippmann attributes to a nationalism that overcame the particularism of petty states. This inclusive nationalism which led to political unification reached its height during the period between the decline of mercantilism and its revival, between about 1776 and 1870. Free trade flourished, reformers aimed toward emancipation, toward abolishing privilege and limiting the power of the state. About 1870 the reaction set in. With the decline of the liberal philosophy, there came renewed authoritarianism, political disunion (a centrifugal tendency), and divisiveness instead of unity and greater liberty. Collectivism is the great villain, for "authoritarianism divides [where] liberalism unites." This is most clearly evident in the "realistic, full-blown collectivists—Stalin, Musso-

---

[16] Ibid., pp. 112–113, 122–130.

lini, Hitler"—but everywhere "collectivism moves toward autar-
chy, the totalitarian states toward isolation."[17]

The liberalism of the nineteenth century meant, or made possible, collective security. It ended "the threat of total wars for
supremacy," for it did away with the privileges that gave supremacy its value. When political power was unimportant, it influenced men's lives very little. But when governments began
to deal again in matters of commerce and trade, ownership and
earnings, supremacy became a matter of paramount importance,
and no longer was there peace sporadically disrupted by local
upheavals. Once supremacy becomes an issue, there is an ongoing
state of war interrupted now and then by periods of apparent
peace.[18]

The revival of massive wars has occurred when many had come
to believe that wars are an anachronism. So begins Chapter IX,
"The Great Revolution and the Rise of the Great Society." If this
is the attitude of most men, why the wars of almost unprecedented destructiveness? If men of the nineteenth century saw war as
utterly contrary to reason and morality, why have men of the
twentieth century engaged in this grim and destructive pastime?
Surely none since such civil wars as the Thirty Years' War in
Germany and the American Civil War (an exception to the generally minor affairs of its century) have been so nearly total in
destructiveness as the First and Second World Wars (the latter
two of course on a vastly larger scale). The answer seems to lie
in the reversal of the trend toward interdependence and the division of labor among nations as within nations. The collectivist
counterrevolutions of the left and of the right are attempts to
counteract the results of the progressive division of labor. Men
have ceased to see in the free market the prime regulator, one that
does far better what the planning board is supposed to do in a
planned economy. They no longer accept the doctrine that the
foundation of liberty is preservation and perfection of the free

[17] Ibid., pp. 132–140.
[18] Ibid., pp. 154–155.

market. For this concept they have substituted faith in regulation by authority.[19]

Adam Smith was a true, if a limited prophet. He recognized increased division of labor as genuinely revolutionary, as radical and far-reaching in its implications as the change from hunting and gathering to established agriculture. Karl Marx failed to see that the radical aspect of the industrial revolution was to be found in technology and economic practices. His interpretation of the nature of the new industrial system confused the permanent and fundamental change brought about by the division of labor and the relative transience of existing political and economic institutions. Because of this confusion he was a "false prophet," even a reactionary, preaching an old and outmoded doctrine in a new and emerging society. His doctrine strikes at the fundamental division of labor and calls for a "reactionary political method to deal with the problems of a progressive economy."[20] Marx misled those who followed him in seeking to deal with the gross inequities of early industrialism. Instead of teaching them that the answer lay in the development of a free market with increasing division of labor through free trade, he taught them that the division of labor could be controlled by omnipotent administration from above. When Lenin first came to power, he administered a socialist economy simply by officially recording labor and products. What saved Lenin and his regime was war and scarcity; the result was centralized control that was totally unrelated to the teachings of Marx. Production in that planned economy has been determined by hunger and military requirements. Russia, like all totalitarian regimes, must somehow reestablish a market economy, once the need for mobilization and the scarcities of famine or near-famine cease to exist. Most of the later liberals shared the errors of Marx. They failed to see that the status quo was not liberalism fully achieved. Consequently the basic conflict between collectivism and liberalism became indistinct. Since

[19] Ibid., pp. 159–174.
[20] Ibid., pp. 177–178.

the existing order was far from satisfactory, such liberals as Herbert Spencer attempted to justify a situation intolerable by any humane standard. As a result their stance became indefensible, their work unproductive.[21]

Liberal philosophy fell into decadence during the century following the publication of Adam Smith's *The Wealth of Nations*, becoming little more than an assortment of "querulous shibboleths" called up to defend vested interests against encroachment. The intellectuals, in criticizing the inequities and injustices of the existing order, employed theories based on socialist principles. The liberal philosophy became empirically absurd. The great error the liberals fell into was exemplified in the debate over laissez faire. They wrote complicated treatises based on the premise that laissez faire was accepted public policy. They made the profound error of thinking that "any aspect of work or of property is ever unregulated by law."[22] It is a grotesque mistake to think that two areas of activity are possible, that of anarchy and that of law. Only on a desert island can man be free without law. The real question, the only question, is what kind of law should exist. While the laissez faire theorists were obscuring the issues with generalizations about the proper extent of the laws, innumerable transactions concerning property and production were being made under the protection of laws made and enforced by society and the courts. Later liberals, such as Herbert Spencer, were intellectually in error in their attempts to define state jurisdiction, for the entire economic system "exists in a legal context, and is inconceivable apart from that context."[23] These liberals appear to have thought of the traditional laws of property and contract as part of the natural order, beyond human question, and of any changes in these laws as intervention by the state, whereas they were in fact upholding a legal system made up of

[21] Ibid., pp. 178–182. Also p. 182, n. 16: "Since 1870 the United States Supreme Court has been a rather consistent exponent of latter-day liberalism."
[22] Ibid., pp. 183–185, 186.
[23] Ibid., pp. 186–189.

bits of ancient law and of new laws that promoted or protected special interests.[24]

The true, the original, liberals had perceived the essence of the method of production brought by the industrial revolution—"the division of labor which transforms more or less self-sufficient men and relatively autonomous communities into a Great Society."[25] In the eighteenth and nineteenth centuries men like Hume and Adam Smith made the tremendous discovery that the good fortune and the prosperity of other nations multiplied that of their own country as a result of the division of labor and freedom of trade. The nineteenth century ranks among the most creative eras. This fact is sometimes obscured by the errors of the economists who fell under the dogma of laissez faire. They drew far-reaching conclusions from the beginnings of something that had so far provided insufficient data. Where Adam Smith was concerned with the promise of the new economic or industrial order, Malthus and Ricardo were concerned with the distribution of wealth, not its production. But the proportion of wealth going to the poor is smaller in undeveloped than in rich and developed societies. Undeveloped societies thus lack the purchasing power required for capitalism to be profitable. The classical economists assumed what was in fact a myth—that man's behavior could be predicted, that labor and capital could easily adapt to different modes of production. Such a society would be governed by "natural values"; competition and opportunity, wisdom and adaptability would be perfect and complete. They had to imagine a society of rational individuals in which perfect justice would come about from the division of labor. Instead of carrying on the tradition of Adam Smith, a critic of the status quo, they became apologists for the existing order, which fell far short of the task of

---

[24] Ibid., pp. 189–191.

[25] Ibid., p. 192. In the footnote on this page Lippmann refers to Wallas's *Great Society*, and adds, "My own *Public Opinion* is a study of democracy in the Great Society; *A Preface to Morals* is a study of certain moral and religious consequence of this transformation." *A Preface to Politics, Drift and Mastery, The Method of Freedom*, and *The New Imperative* are not mentioned.

adjusting accepted practices and institutions to meet the needs of the new industrial system.[26]

There was a great need for reform, but the classical economics, with its laissez faire obsession, was little more than a negative and complaisant defense of the dominant classes. The economists were not hardened men with no sense of justice; they were simply caught in the web of their own dogma, which restrained their sympathy and allowed no hope for improving the human condition. When Adam Smith and Jeremy Bentham were writing, the philosophy of liberalism took the initiative in working social changes to accommodate the new industrialism. By the time of Herbert Spencer it had become a philosophy of negativism and opposition to social change. This may be seen not only in Spencer's later work, but in a number of Supreme Court rulings under the due process clause.[27]

The social problems neglected or even denied by the classical economists of the nineteenth century have many causes, not the single one decried by the socialists, that legal title to property is vested in private persons rather than in the state. While the industrial revolution is still taking place, there can be no static order. Social progress derives from an expanding economy. The enormously complex problems of helping the physically and socially disabled, of mass education, of training specialists without trapping them in their specialty are questions that do not settle themselves. They must be a part of liberal policy. Similarly, the harmful results and the hazards of the business cycle and the fluctuations in the value of money are all matters not automatically regulated by a laissez faire policy; in a period of technical specialization caveat emptor is no longer an adequate rule.[28] No liberal state can remain neutral between the weak, who have nothing to bargain with, and the powerful, who scarcely need

[26] Ibid., pp. 195–201.

[27] Ibid., pp. 203, 208.

[28] Ibid., pp. 210–213, 219–221. In neither of these instances, of course, can the ends Lippmann sets forth be achieved without direction and some control by the state.

bargain at all. The industrial society is dynamic; it is not hardened to human cost. For instance, taxation could be used to protect those who suffer loss as a result of industrial progress. The greater equalization of incomes is an essential and an appropriate objective of a liberal policy "if *brought about in the way outlined here*"—that is, promoting the division of labor through an efficient market economy.[29]

The dole, that is, money given to the needy, is a relief, not a remedy. On the other hand money spent on such projects as public health, education, conservation, and public works "is both a relief and a remedy."[30] Such measures improve the productivity of labor, help to raise the living standard of the people and the nation. Some of the benefits are for the long run, for a generation unborn, and therefore can be expected only of public authority. Evidently this kind of investment in the present and in the future is not the planning to which the author so strongly objects. It is not collectivism, but rather a means of improving the whole economy. Similarly, it is appropriate to correct the maldistribution due to unearned increments by reforms that attack monopolies and forced bargains. Such reforms will not fully equalize, but they will tend to redistribute income. If markets were open and both capital and labor sufficiently mobile, interest rates would decline and the disproportionate distance between the highest and the lowest incomes would be narrowed. This equalization of the distribution of income is greatly to be desired, even though it will not erase or correct all inequities. From the day of Aristotle men have seen that a large and growing middle class is an essential element of a sound and durable society, since extremes of wealth and privation imperil social stability.[31]

All of this Lippmann believes to be part, though not a compre-

---

[29] Ibid., pp. 222–223, 227. Lippmann's advocacy here of far-reaching economic controls to cut the human cost of industrial progress seems in curious contrast to his denunciation of New Deal tactics in the early pages of the book.

[30] Ibid., p. 228.

[31] Ibid., pp. 228–232.

hensive outline, of liberal social reform. The immediate question, to one who has read the first part of his book, is how can it be achieved without planning and government controls? They—these collectivist reforms—are not what the totalitarian states seek to achieve. They "revert . . . to the caste system at home and to depredations against their neighbors." The essential distinction is that the collectivists would deny the interdependence that the division of labor has fostered among men. Where "liberalism seeks to improve the exchange economy . . . collectivism would abolish it. Liberalism is radical in relation to the social order but conservative in relation to the division of labor in a market economy."[32] Liberalism then is not that advocated by Herbert Spencer, but that of the critical and reforming spirit of Adam Smith.

In Chapter XII, "The Political Principles of Liberalism," the author reverts to the view that between 1600 and 1800 progressives strove to establish the basic security necessary for a successful market economy. This included bringing kings under the law and attacking economic piracy, whether on the high seas or in the houses of state, ensuring that laws of property and contract would be honored in all ways necessary to guarantee the security of economic transaction. It was the feeling behind these reforms that led liberals to the passionate belief in the natural and inviolable rights of contract and property. This was a myth, a "vital lie," and the liberals really did not mean that these rights were beyond control; they meant rather that the power of the state ought to be devoted to protecting the integrity of the rights of property and contract. When their ideas were evolving, the state did not meet this need adequately. When the commercial classes became the controlling power in government, they were responsible for finding in the law the guarantee of social needs, of what were coming to be called natural rights.[33] A closer study of bills of rights in England and America in the seventeenth and eighteenth centuries might have diluted the author's generalization here, but he is correct in saying that property and usually the

[32] Ibid., pp. 234–236.
[33] Ibid., pp. 242–243.

right to contract (though this came later in its fully developed form) were among the natural rights.

Important as the conception of natural and inviolable rights was in dissolving ancient restrictions and securing the protection of property and contract, it came to stand in the way of needed change, for it obscured the fact that not only governments, but also corporations and business transactions come under the law and that property rights are limited by law and may be modified by law. Thus in the seventeenth-century struggle against the Stuarts an incomplete theory of liberties was forged. It sought limitations on the powers of the monarchy but did not work a theory for adaptation to changing circumstances.

More important was the work of the American revolutionists, who renounced both monarchy and hereditary aristocracy and relied upon the active consent, as well as the power, of all men. What they undertook was without doubt the most important political experiment of the modern era. Luckily they were men of unusual political ability and discernment; they perceived the basic political problem of a liberal social system, even if they were unable to complete its solution. Their task was not simply to abridge royal authority, but to give shape and force to government by the people. In formulating a system of government based solely upon the consent of the governed, the Americans of 1776–1789 "made a contribution to the science of government which is the necessary premise of all political thinking in the modern world."[34] They did not make the mistake of believing that the people understood how to govern, though they had the right to govern. The problem as they saw it was enabling the people to govern. The grand conception of the United States Constitution is its description of the way in which diffuse popular power can be concentrated and shaped into effective government. It is neither the only nor a perfect system, but the fundamental question cannot be avoided; the leaders of the Revolution faced it directly. The urgency of the question is perhaps stronger today than it was

[34] Ibid., pp. 247–248.

then.[35] The authors of the Constitution did not theorize naively about democracy; they considered the will of the people to be the balance of its many parts. They did not go in for "cynical plebiscites," or for what some later theorists of pure democracy favor— simple majority rule, ignoring the necessity of considering the interests and rights of minorities and the equal necessity of more searching discussion of complex issues than is possible in the kind of mass voting so easily misled by demagogues. "James Madison would not have been astonished by Hitler."[36] His historical studies had made him aware of the dangers of demagogues, and he sought to prevent the republic from going the way of nearly all republics of which he had read. That is why he, and the other founders, sought to establish a genuinely representative government. If the Constitution's system of checks and balances (less comprehensive, by the way, than that of the most democratically adopted state constitution—the Massachusetts Constitution of 1780) has become outmoded, other checks on the dangers of mob rule must be worked out.

Lippmann goes on to describe how additional limitations were imposed on the national government—the Bill of Rights (far briefer than those of several Revolutionary state constitutions) and such conceptions as Marshall's view in *Fletcher* vs. *Peck* (1810) that the Georgia statute was contrary not to particular provisions of the Constitution, but to the "general principles which are common to our institutions." Marshall did invoke this general conception, but he invoked it as a support to his enlarged theory of the obligation of the contract clause, and by 1812 the "general principles" had been dropped as unnecessary. Nor is it made clear that Justice Holmes's protest (in *Lochner* vs. *New York*, 1905) "that the Fourteenth Amendment does not enact Mr. Herbert Spencer's *Social Statics*" was against the scope given, not to the contract clause, but to the due process clause of the Fourteenth Amendment. In this and other contract and especially due process cases, the judges "lost their understanding of the great

[35] Ibid., pp. 250–251.
[36] Ibid., pp. 253–255, 256.

political discovery which inspired the original Constitution" (that the function of a constitution is to refine the will of the people) and tried to establish judicial rules to restrain that will. The courts and the beneficiaries of their decisions produced a clash between the greater part of the voting populace and those who wanted to check the power of the people. These men "fell into a tragic error when they failed to hold fast to the original insight of the Constitution: that it is upon the refinement of the popular will that a progressive society must depend."[37]

Belief in democracy has from the beginning kept uneasy company in America with attempts to inhibit democracy in action. Lippmann states that by 1936 the Republicans had "become the ardent disciples of Thomas Jefferson and James Madison."[38] This is clearly wrong to anyone who will look at the record. Jefferson and Madison did take the lead in the 1798–1799 Kentucky and Virginia resolutions, which were the only available means of protesting the bad Alien, and the indefensible Sedition acts (the lower federal courts had upheld the acts against critics of the Adams administration), and Jefferson was always against the Hamiltonian finance program, which he saw as an early Wall Street. But it is equally true that Madison in the Federal Convention wanted a stronger central government than the one adopted, that the second war with England was called Mr. Madison's war and was bitterly unpopular among states'-rights Federalists in New England, that he signed the charter of the Second Bank of the United States in 1816. Jefferson sought extraordinary powers under the Articles of Confederation (even to ending slavery in all the western territories), declared before 1787 that the Union must be strengthened, was a life-long advocate of reforms in Virginia, many unacceptably radical for their day, bought Louisiana without constitutional authority, asked for amendments to enable the national government to aid in public works, especially interstate roads, and education, including a national university. It is evident that the American theory of popular government has

[37] Ibid., pp. 257, 259, 260.
[38] Ibid., p. 261.

not been a mass or plebiscitary democracy, but it is not correct to line up the leaders as Lippmann does. And it does not clarify the complexities to say that the original doctrine was that the people were not expected to decide much or often (except in New England town meetings), that we have inherited an idea of democracy that, though based upon representation, "is without guiding principles as to how the people shall legislate."[39]

Lippmann's interpretation of our history is that, since there was no theory of how to govern, the people's representatives drew upon the ideas they inherited from the kings, which meant corruption, bureaucracy, inefficiency, the increase in the number of officials and in their power. Progressives advocated a strong state, reactionaries stood firm for individual rights; the doctrines later became collectivism and laissez faire. But this conflict is false and obscures the true answer—a society regulated, not by overhead control, but by a common law that sets forth the complementary rights and duties of individuals and enables them to compel observance of the law through litigation.[40] This sounds like a splendid way out until we realize that it is shifting the burden of needed changes from executive and legislative bodies to courts, which are not adequately equipped to deal with most of them.

Lippmann has earlier made clear that the great changes in technology, in transportation, communications, and the scale of industry in the nineteenth century brought unprecedented difficulties with them. Surely the ancient system of the common law, admirable as it is in many ways, cannot cope with them. In many instances the courts can do little more than decide whether nation or state, or neither, shall regulate. It is no solution to say that "thus in a free society the state does not administer the affairs of men. It administers justice among men who conduct their own affairs."[41] According to what rules is justice determined when the courts begin to deal with entirely unprecedented methods of transportation, with commercial enterprise on a scale and in

[39] Ibid., p. 263.
[40] Ibid., pp. 263–266.
[41] Ibid., p. 267.

forms unknown to Coke and Blackstone—or to Marshall and Kent? But Lippmann insists that the nineteenth-century conflict between the anarchy of property owners and the collectivist theory of management by public officials is wrong. Recognition of only the two alternatives came about through inaccurate observation and inadequate analysis; it overlooks the vast area covered by the evolution of private rights and duties enforceable in the courts. To talk of laissez faire is deceptive; collectivism is unacceptable. Property rights can and should be regulated and changed as needed, but this does not require state, that is, collective, control. It means readjustment of the rights of citizens with each other, and the enforcing agency is the courts. This is as true for giant corporations as for the property rights of private individuals. There are no grounds for assuming, as advocates of both individualism and collectivism do, that corporations can operate only in one or the other extreme state—within their present freedom or under complete government control.[42]

"The Government of a Liberal State" (Chapter XIII) begins with the assertion that the chances for freedom in the future will depend upon whether men in a position to lead can look for the solution of social and economic problems "by the readjustment of private rights rather than by public administration." That leaves out most of the major problems of the last two generations, but Lippmann clearly believes that in the law he has discovered the clue to the recovery of the liberalism of Adam Smith. He has previously cited the misuse of due process by the Supreme Court as an erroneous interpretation of economic and juridical theory and practice, but he asserts and reasserts that justice in the liberal state is maintained by dispensing justice among individuals instead of directing men's affairs from above.[43] I think it is generally true that the state and national legislative bodies of the period he is writing about were more concerned with justice, social and economic, than were the courts, but Lippmann is on the side of the judges compared with the legislatures and executives. The

42 Ibid., pp. 268–281.
43 Ibid., pp. 282, 284.

nonjudicial departments are too prone to forget that they are only judges among contending interests; they often fail to remember that law-making is as much a judicial action as ruling on cases under the laws. Legislators have begun to consider themselves "lineal descendants of the Caesars, and the heirs of their sovereignty. Against this revival of the absolute state, the courts have sought to provide a refuge."[44] He gives no examples here, but one wonders which line of decisions he has in mind, those relating to labor (where the courts commonly stood against legislative aid to the workers before 1937), income taxes (the Pollock case of 1895 was, in the phrase of Charles Evans Hughes, one of the three self-inflicted wounds of the Supreme Court's history), or interpretations of the commerce clause that favored big business but prevented the abolition of the worst forms of child labor.[45]

If Lippmann is writing of his own country, not of Russia, Italy, or Germany, it is not helpful to an understanding of the four decades before 1937 to say that liberalism governs through ensuring reciprocating rights and duties, authoritarianism by decree. Were the legislative attempts to deal with existing evils in labor relations, corporate monopolies and conspiracies, or tax inequities decrees, or were the judicial vetoes of these statutes more accurately so described? In these pages it seems almost as if the author is, in spite of earlier statements about the need for change and adaptation, thinking in terms of small-scale enterprise, before the technological innovations of the late nineteenth and early twentieth centuries brought alterations of a magnitude that required some degree and kind of legislative regulation.

It is easy to agree that what Lippmann keeps referring to as the "authoritarian system" is effective in times of crisis, especially in times of war. But is it so clear that individual miners and great steel or mining corporations meet as individuals? Bureaucracy flourishes in time of war (as does waste on a colossal scale), but are social regulations enacted by legislatures inevitably in the

[44] Ibid., pp. 287–288.
[45] See Benjamin F. Wright, *Growth of American Constitutional Law*, chs. VIII, IX.

same category? Are they all to be seen as enemies of a free society? The discussion at times seems to see the society of 1937 as one
of equal individuals or at least of individuals equally able to bring
their grievances or causes for disagreement to the courts or to
bargaining between men. The Supreme Court, earlier criticized
for its due process decisions (which were reversed beginning in
the year this book was published), is here given as an example of
an agency that decides specific controversies, not as an example of
overhead control by authoritarian official force.[46]

Government suited to human capacity means government
limited to questions of particular, immediate problems of justice,
not the devising and ordering of aims, designs, and administration
of a future social order. Ordinary men may be able to determine
in specific instances what is just or unjust, but it is not possible for
men to plan and administer the social order. The result of so ambitious and ill-conceived a program is the inescapable conflict of
specific interests. The liberal conception of the state is one
wrought out empirically during the centuries in which the English common law and constitutional practice were developed. This
is far different from the conceptions of either Rousseau or the
Jacobins. The great error was made when the democrats began to
look to the state, not as the source of justice, but as the source
of abundant life. Government has to be limited to man's capabili-
ties—to the dispensing of justice. This seems to come down to
decisions made in the light of general rules that can be improved
if justice demands it; the chief need of an official is therefore an
ability to evaluate evidence. In an authoritarian state there can be
no appeal against irremediable wrongs.[47]

This distinction does not mean an acceptance of the callous opposition of Herbert Spencer, for example, to public health measures because they interfered with human liberty. But it does
mean that as public enterprises increase in number and in scale,
there is greater necessity for governmental authority to arbitrate

[46] Lippmann, *The Good Society*, p. 293.
[47] Ibid., pp. 294–297.

in conflicts between public and private interests, even among the different government enterprises. The great problem with the increase of public programs is not their basic purposes, but the difficulty of regulating the power of bureaucracies, which tend to assume imperial attributes. The single defense against the arbitrary rule of officials is to limit their jurisdiction to specifically defined areas.[48]

Lippmann admits readily that the vastly greater increase in economic affairs, both in size and complexity, makes for differences from the legal order of the seventeenth or eighteenth centuries. But, granted the changes and the inevitable increase in functions of the liberal states and the fact that technical matters require the attention of experts, it is as unquestionable now as in the early days of the law merchant that the markets cannot be effectively regulated by the legislative body. The more that is delegated to administrators, the greater becomes the necessity for review of their actions. Otherwise the representative state will have placed the management of its affairs in the hands of an irresponsible bureaucracy. It is of the essence of a liberal society that its officials be held responsible and their actions reviewable, especially in the courts. The judiciary, firmly condemned for its due process rulings, and clearly distrusted in *A Preface to Politics*, is now seen as the great source of protection. This is not consistent, however, with the statement that only through the "representative state" can the affairs of individuals and of corporations be governed.[49] By representative state we would ordinarily understand elected legislators and executives, though Rousseau thought otherwise.

It is inconceivable that a sovereign—"be it a man, an oligarchy, or a ruling party in colored shirts"—could rule over all mankind. It follows that government by an overhead agency, admittedly effective in a society of limited size and development, is practicable in a larger, complex society only in times of crisis. Moreover,

[48] Ibid., pp. 298–300.
[49] Ibid., pp. 301–308.

the events of our own time have taught us that a state-controlled economy, always complete in itself and always militarized, is not conducive to peace at home or abroad.[50]

The socialized administered states "have confused law which comes from the usages of the people with the governing power which comes from the prerogatives of conquerors and masters." The valid law that makes for justice and peace does not come from the centralization of a powerful bureaucracy.[51]

At places in *The Good Society* the author seems to be condemning all forms of legislative control, or the delegating to administrators of the power to carry out legislation, in the western constitutional democracies as in the socialist or fascist states. In the section in Chapter XIV on the civil society, however, we are told that the western democracies, including Argentina, have substantially the same rule of law. The peoples of these countries "transact their affairs under laws which are not identical but are fundamentally similar, and . . . are administered impartially to citizens and aliens alike." It is in the totalitarian states that one is at the mercy of official discretion, with no recourse in law.[52]

Then comes the surprising prophecy: "In the end no nation can fail to enter this system where common law prevails: if it is backward, unable or unwilling to make its portion of the earth secure for the new economy of the division of labor, its certain destiny is to be conquered. Unless it is as remote as Tibet, in one way or another it will be brought within the necessary jurisdiction of the Great Society."[53] We can hope that this forecast of things to come is more accurate than Lippmann's earlier remark about the impracticality of a war of movement or his statement, when discussing the necessity of a division of labor and of a common law throughout the world, that "no one has planned the conquest of Holland or of Scandinavia." Two of the Scandinavian countries, along with Holland, were conquered three years after the book

[50] Ibid., pp. 313–315.
[51] Ibid., p. 316.
[52] Ibid., p. 318.
[53] Ibid., pp. 319, 321.

was published, and by a totalitarian power on its way to European centralization and control, an ambition very nearly achieved.

A more accurate generalization, though one can find exceptions, is that the rule of peace coincides with a social order in which there is equality under the law. Trouble breaks out in areas that have yet to establish this kind of society.[54] There are a good many other factors involved (religious unity or religious toleration and the acceptance of an established method of transferring power are examples), but the point is an important one.

The struggle for law is not, if peace and order and justice are to be secured, a search or struggle for absolute power for rulers, or even for majorities. The struggle for absolute power "is the turbulence of this modern world, and the indeterminateness of the promises is its moral and intellectual confusion." The "cardinal heresy of the modern generation" is "the idea of arbitrary power exercised at the willful discretion of any man." This is the "legalism of barbarism."[55] It is foreign to civilization.

All civilized societies have professed a belief in a universal law above the laws and customs of men. This conception, which has taken various forms, has been argued as long as men have argued general ideas. Generally it has been invoked by the weak to challenge the arbitrary power of the strong. This higher and more universal law has been appealed to against slavery, in the efforts to establish constitutional government and to protect human rights and free markets.[56] (It was also invoked by the defenders of slavery in the South, especially after 1831.)

Certainly there have been many and important appeals to natural law, as by the great Roman jurists and by St. Thomas Aquinas, but appeals to the natural rights of individuals or of the governed against their governors are rare before the Reformation. Contrary to what Lippmann says, such appeal has not been *the* security against either tyranny or, what is very different indeed, anarchy. Nor is it self-evident that "a free and ordered society,

54 Ibid., pp. 322–323.
55 Ibid., pp. 331–332.
56 Ibid., p. 334.

resting chiefly on persuasion rather than on coercion . . . is in-conceivable in theory and unworkable in practice unless in the community there is a general willingness to be bound by the spirit of a law that is higher and more universal than the letter of particular laws." As Lippmann indicates, though not clearly, the high point in the long history of this conception was reached in the eighteenth century. Critics of natural law from Hume and Bentham to Pareto are as misguided as those conservatives who have identified the higher law with their vested interests. Lipp-mann asserts that the doctrine dear to the philosophers and jurists of the past and to the fathers of constitutional government relied upon an intuition, often inadequately expressed, which reflects a striving of the human soul essential to national and international order and peace.[57]

The classic examples he gives of the value of a higher, or na-tural, law are drawn largely from the struggle over authority and the succession in England in the seventeenth century. His heroes in the controversy are Coke and Selden. Locke, classic defender of the Glorious Revolution of 1688, is not mentioned, nor is Milton or Sydney. Curiously, there is here almost nothing about the American Revolution, either the English or the American Bill of Rights.[58] It is indeed strange that an American author seeking to find the basis for the rule of law and the protection of the rights of individuals should stop with Coke and Sir Thomas Smith, an ambassador and a secretary to Queen Elizabeth, and not even mention the English Bill of Rights of 1689, much less such earlier American colonial documents as the Massachusetts Body of Lib-erties of 1641, which went beyond it in several important respects.

The penultimate chapter, "The Pursuit of Liberty," begins with the proposition that negative restraints on power are essential but that the pursuit of liberty is more than that. Liberalism is not laissez faire, the unlimited right of the strong to acquire and to control. Liberalism has meant rebellion against oppression, against aggression and acquisitiveness. It is found in the develop-

[57] Ibid., pp. 335, 337.
[58] Ibid., pp. 338–342.

ment of law, the definition of rights and duties. Law must be strong enough to restrain aggressors at home and abroad. It is in such a condition that the creative faculties can function. When the talented and the accomplished are reduced by authority that controls opinion and brings the cultural level of all the people down to that of the politicians in power, the liberal society is doomed. Liberalism does not mean equality for all in wealth, wisdom, or authority, but rather removal of the extrinsic inequalities so that intrinsic ability can emerge.[59] In isolated and economically primitive societies, there is no need for constitutional liberty, and the notion only rarely arises. It does appear among those who, from the time of Athens and Rome to the present, trading widely with other peoples, have conceived the good life and the necessity for law. The contemporary authoritarians who yearn for closed systems and planned national economies have produced a world economy that displays less order and regularity than most that have existed in the past. The present condition is neither systematic nor even organized. Those in authority can do no more than judge among conflicting interests and ease the conflicts of competition by making justice under the law increasingly equitable.[60]

No benevolent despot could comprehend or manage this vast and complicated economy. The collectivist planners do not deal with man as he exists, but with some altogether different being. Their plans call for superhuman qualities of intelligence and virtue. Liberalism, the Good Society, offers no blueprints for perfection. Such ordered plans or designs can no more be realized in the modern world than Plato's Republic could exist outside Plato's imagination. The "testament of liberty" is not a design for a new social order. The liberal state guards against inequity and arbitrariness by administering justice among individuals. Liberalism entrusts the fate of civilization, not to a handful of powerful but mortal men, but to "the whole genius of mankind. This is a grander vision than that of those who would be Caesar and would set

[59] Ibid., pp. 352–358.
[60] Ibid., pp. 361–363.

themselves up as little tin gods over men."[61] It is also, though Lippmann does not seem to realize it, a retreat into mysticism.

The final chapter, "On This Rock," is essentially a reiteration of the view that the foundations of tyranny lie in the regimentation of men, that centralized planning and forcible direction of human affairs from above were fundamentally antagonistic to natural implications of the division of labor. The author's study of past achievements and current tyrannies had led to the conviction that the division of labor, democracy, and the common law are so related that they must stand or fall together. In the latter part of the nineteenth century Adam Smith was applauded, but in practice the reaction was against the sanctity of the individual. The iconoclasts mistook knowledge for wisdom, rationalism for reason, the enchantment of a new and undeveloped science for the reality of established truths. Among men of intellect there was a lack of respect for man himself. As a result, the ideals of justice, freedom, and brotherhood were abandoned as superstitions, like the notions of the Almighty, the immortality of the soul, and the divine law. These thinkers, who sought to analyze man's behavior, have debased the idea of man. This is true of such disparate groups as the followers of Hegel and Marx, the pseudo-Darwinians, and the Spenglerians. Liberalism was, to Nietzsche, the "morality of slaves"; to others it was gross materialism, an opiate for the people, useless sentimentality, or the dogma of a particular group or period of religion or class. All the absolutists met on common ground: "they agreed that freedom of the individual is incompatible with their system."[62]

The foundations of tyranny lie in regimentation. Those who would regiment include not only Marx, Lenin, Stalin, and Hitler but such almost-forgotten reformers as Stuart Chase. Indeed, freedom has fallen victim, almost universally, to reactionism. Promises of peace and plenty, for which men exchanged their liberty and their human dignity, have not been kept. Why not?

[61] Ibid., pp. 363–368.
[62] Ibid., pp. 373–374, 379–382.

Because collectivism, apparently that of the western democracies as well as that of the totalitarian states, is incapable of regulating by law the contradictory social interests within the modern economy. Reverting to the primitive idea of government by coercion, it gives new life to the age-old parochial enmities of man.[63]

Collectivism may be temporarily triumphant, but it will ultimately fail, because it is founded on an utterly false idea of the nature of the economy, of the law, of sovereignty, of man himself. The hope for salvation lies in the discontent and the energy that have fought heresies and tyrannies in the past. "For the will to be free is perpetually renewed in every individual who uses his faculties and affirms his manhood."[64]

Essays in the Public Philosophy

In 1955 Lippmann published what has been to date his final systematic book of political theory. With a few exceptions it is a continuation and supplement to *The Good Society* (1937). In the first sentence of *The Public Philosophy*, as the book is almost always referred to, he says that he began the book in the summer of 1938 "in an effort to come to terms in my own mind and heart with the mounting disorder in our Western society."[65] There is greater emphasis in *The Public Philosophy* upon political than upon economic failures, but there is no fundamental change in point of view. There is, however, less inclination to single out the failure of freedom in Russia, Italy, Germany, or other totalitarian states. Spain is barely mentioned, just possibly because it did not suffer from the failings of the Western democracies, and neither China nor Japan is mentioned in either book.

Not the failure to achieve a liberal regime in the Communist countries, which by 1955 made up approximately half the popula-

---

[63] Ibid., pp. 387–388.
[64] Ibid., pp. 388–389.
[65] Walter Lippmann, *The Public Philosophy*, p. 3.

tion of the world, or the Franco dictatorship in Spain, but the fact that the Western democracies did not solve the problems of this century is the central argument of the book. These countries "were now threatened by the rising tide of barbarity" and the liberties won by "centuries of struggle," the "great traditions of civility," are in danger.[66] It was not easy for Lippmann, who had known a gentler world unravaged by global war, "to recognize and acknowledge the sickness of the Western liberal democracies . . . [the] deep disorder in our society which comes not from the machinations of our enemies and from the adversities of the human condition but from within ourselves."[67] Fittingly, Book One has the title, "The Decline of the West."

How far the author had gone in writing the book before December of 1941, when he put aside the incomplete manuscript, is not made clear, but it was certainly not completed and published until ten years after the Second World War was dramatically halted, if not finally ended. He acknowledges that the liberal democracies had defeated their enemies, but "they had been unable to make peace out of their victories." The obvious fact that a nonliberal, nondemocracy, the Soviet Union, had contributed largely to the defeat of Germany and to the disorders of the next decade is not here mentioned, though he does go on to say that prior to 1917 liberal democracies of Britain, France, and the United States provided the model for any new government. It was during that year that the exhaustion of the democracies led to revolution and disorder in Russia and in Germany and Austria-Hungary and to subtle alteration of the constitutional order in the West.[68]

During the century between Waterloo and 1914 governments rarely had to make hard decisions. Except for the American Civil War there were only a few brief local outbreaks of hostility. Released from the terrible necessities of war and peace, governments were free to concern themselves with improvements. Life seemed

[66] Ibid.
[67] Ibid., pp. 4–5.
[68] Ibid., pp. 5–6.

secure, liberty and the pursuit of happiness were generally available.[69]

One of the characteristics of this book is illustrated in the paragraph just summarized. The "hard decisions" are those involving war and peace, not those involving the inequities and the miserable living and working conditions suffered by many, often a majority, of the citizens of the industrialized or industrializing Western countries in the nineteenth century, as well as by the great majority of peoples in nonindustrialized parts of the world. It was a century of social protest and of extremely significant reforms, a very large proportion of them carried out by legislation and against the bitter opposition of the rich and their spokesmen, including such superficially unprejudiced scholars as Sir Henry Maine and Herbert Spencer.[70] Lippmann does write about improvements and of a progressive society, but his emphasis clearly is on the growing weakness of government in this internationally easy century. The softness of democracy—not the reasons for the mass of social and economic criticism, whether the caricatures of Charles Dickens, the numerous social utopias, or the harsh communism of Marx and Engels—is the theme. Even the end of slavery in the West is only casually referred to. This softness led to disaster in 1917, the year of the two Russian revolutions and of the American involvement in the European war. As a result of a greatly weakened executive in the advanced nations, the democracies grew incapable of waging wars of rational purpose, and of making just and lasting peace.[71]

Announcing that he is a "liberal democrat" who has "no wish to disenfranchise [his] fellow citizens," Lippmann nevertheless expresses his profound concern for the last century or more. Later in the book the decline appears to have begun in 1789, the year of the outbreak of the French Revolution and also the year the present American Constitution became the law of the land. Mass

[69] Ibid., p. 9.

[70] See the quotations from Maine on the failings of democracy, ibid., pp. 8, 47.

[71] Ibid., p. 13.

control has succeeded the loss of power by governments, yet a mass is unable to rule. "Where mass opinion dominates the government, there is a morbid derangement of the true functions of power."[72] Lippmann's brooding concern for the decline of the democracies applies to those very countries which did not go through the political convulsions of the last half century—Britain, the United States, the Low Countries, and Scandinavia—as contrasted with those where constitutional democracy had not been long and successfully established—Germany, Austria (or Austria-Hungary, as it was before 1918), Russia, Italy, Spain, and, to a lesser degree, France. The mass democracies, in his opinion, have made critically wrong decisions because "the people have imposed a veto upon the judgments of the informed and responsible officials." In matters of life and death importance, popular opinion has proved to be a "dangerous master of decisions."[73] That mistakes were made, as in the Versailles Treaty, few are likely to deny. Whether the masses, or popular opinions, are primarily responsible, or alternatively, whether the popular views were the result, to use Madison's phrase in the tenth *Federalist*, of "an attachment to different leaders ambitiously contending for preeminence and power," is another question. Perhaps there is, in Lippmann's view, no difference, since he is clear that the failure to make a durable peace was the weakness of statesmanship that came from the necessity to incite the populace to fear, hatred, and dreams of utopian solutions. Similarly in the Second World War, the people had to be promised that with the unconditional surrender of Germany and Japan would come the world-wide triumph of the Four Freedoms. As the people have gained sovereignty the governments have been weakened, have lost the ability to ready themselves for either peace or war. The complexities of the times call for experience and knowledge of circumstances, which invariably are distorted when presented as simple and dogmatic absolutes. The men who warned against these errors

[72] Ibid., pp. 13–15.
[73] Ibid., p. 20.

usually went unheard or were defeated. The very survival of society when the great issues of war and peace, of revolution and order are up for decision is endangered if the executive and judicial departments, with their civil servants and technicians, have lost their power to decide.[74]

The immediate answer to this decline of government in the liberal democracies is a return to a stronger executive, a frank recognition that when such great questions are at stake, the legislature must not be allowed to exercise the power of the executive.[75] Is it irrelevant to compare the record of the Western democracies with the dictatorships (strong executives, certainly not mass democracies) of Stalin, Mussolini, Hitler, and Franco? It is true that in the major democracies of the West there were often weak executives, or perhaps one can more accurately say ineffective men, in high executive office in the decades between the two great wars. Would Lippmann have so exalted the executive power had he been writing of the administrations of Buchanan and Grant? He did not do so in the three books which were published in the time of Harding and Coolidge.

Lippmann's argument for greater or more effective power in the executive is not a simple one. It is not confined to the statements that "the executive is the active power in the state, the asking and the proposing power. The representative assembly is the consenting power, the petitioning, the approving and the criticizing, the accepting and the refusing power. The two powers are necessary if there is to be order and freedom."[76]

There follows a somewhat confusing section, "The People and the Voters." Near its beginning Lippmann says flatly that "the Western liberal democracies are a declining power in human affairs." I am not certain how this relates to his argument for an increase in the power of the executive, partly because he uses the

74 Ibid., pp. 21–25, 27. On page 26 there is a quotation from James Truslow Adams, *The Adams Family* (1930), which contains praise of Washington, Hamilton, and John Adams, who "refused to truckle to the people."
75 Lippmann, *Public Philosophy*, p. 30.
76 Ibid.

historical argument that the opening phrase of the Constitution, "We the people," did not in fact mean the mass of the people. The Constitution was adopted by a restricted electorate, presumably a small minority of the adult free males, except in New York.[77] He gives the impression of regretting expansion of the suffrage and the consequent decision of major issues on the basis of mass prejudices or opinions, of disavowing Bentham's idea that the common interest of a society is simply the sum of all those individual interests present in the given society at any given time. Lippmann clearly prefers Burke's conception of the community as one continuing entity or organism. Just how this community is to be represented is left vague, but twentieth-century plebiscites have not been the answer. His conclusion is "that public opinion becomes less realistic as the mass to whom information must be conveyed, and argument must be addressed, grows larger and more heterogeneous."[78] Just as the Constitution of 1787 preceded by two generations or more the mass electorates of the twentieth century, so the British Bill of Rights antedates by two centuries Britain's universal suffrage. He believes that this historical fact is disconcerting to present-day liberals because it apparently demonstrates that the mass of electors have not been the most steadfast defenders of freedom.[79]

Chapter IV of this appeal to the virtues and achievements of

[77] Ibid., pp. 31–33. Lippmann's account of the 1787–1788 ratification is no longer accepted by most historians. He is clearly in error about several states. In Massachusetts, for example, not only did nearly all men have the vote (see Robert E. Brown, Middle Class Democracy in Massachusetts, 1691–1780), but further, the experience of that state in which one proposed state constitution had been rejected by the voters in town meetings, and another, that of 1780, accepted after the same intensive examination, made for an awareness of and an interest in constitutional ratification well beyond that usually found in recent times.

[78] Ibid., pp. 35, 39.

[79] Ibid., p. 40. Whether the majority have generally supported greater freedom for all is debatable, and answers have varied from time to time and place to place. What is certain is that the legal protection for the civil liberties of all men in the United States was greatly expanded during the latter part of the period he is discussing.

the past is entitled "The Public Interest." It displays a very low opinion of public polls as instruments for ascertaining that interest. How then can we determine and judge the public interest? The answer is surprisingly close to that of Plato's *Republic* and even closer to Rousseau's in the *Social Contract*: "the public interest may be presumed to be what men would choose if they saw clearly, thought rationally, acted disinterestedly and benevolently."[80] Plato's proposed method was an elaborate and protracted system of education, as well as a system of communism for guardians and warriors (not for the mass of men). The elusive Rousseau is not that clear about the means of discovering the general will, nor is Lippmann. What is evident is that the decline of the West has been caused in large part by giving in to mass prejudices and pressures, by failure of strong executive leadership. "There is then a general tendency to be drawn downward, as by the force of gravity, towards insolvency, towards the insecurity of factionalism, towards the erosion of liberty, and towards hyperbolic wars."[81]

The next chapter opens with a sympathetic reference to Sir Henry Maine's statement, made in 1866, that one can find "little" in the history of modern popular government "to support the assumption that popular government has an indefinitely long future before it.... it is characterized by great fragility, and... since its appearance, all forms of government have become more insecure than they were before."[82] The weakening of the executive power is to Lippmann the cause of that fragility. But so much emphasis upon the decline of executive power not only exaggerates far too much but also omits other factors at least as significant in the developments he deplores.

The sections on the protection of the executive and the voters and the executive (pp. 49–54) are irritating because they are, with few exceptions, historically wrong. The executives in the

---

80 Ibid., p. 42.
81 Ibid., p. 46.
82 Ibid., p. 47. The quotation is from Maine's *Popular Government* (1886), p. 20.

states become stronger, not weaker, with the growth of popular rule, including the broadening of the suffrage. Although the first group of state constitutions, those of 1776, all provided for governors elected by the legislatures, the trend toward more independent executives with greater powers began with the New York Constitution of 1777 and was carried on in Massachusetts in 1780, in New Hampshire in 1784, and in many others during the era of the "rise of the common man." The references to the protection of the executive in the Constitution of 1787, discussed by Madison and by Hamilton (in the forty-eighth and forty-ninth and the seventy-first *Federalists*, respectively),[83] reflect the tendency both in the states and in such criticisms of the 1776 constitutions' inadequate separation of powers as Jefferson's *Notes on Virginia*.

The conclusion of this section states ambitiously, if vaguely, a principle that gets at the basic problem of modern democracy. Elected officials owe less allegiance to the opinions of the voters than to law, to their professional standards, to their consciousness of duty under rules of order they have vowed to obey and defend. Once the ruler is elected, he is responsible primarily to his office rather than to his electors. Apparently the election of an executive differs fundamentally from that of a representative. An executive cannot be merely the instrument of those who elect him whereas a representative should be substantially that. Effective representation of the voters is necessary to the liberty and order of a civil society, "but representation must not be confused with voting." The "democratic disaster" of recent times has been caused by the confusion of government, the act of administering and initiating law, with representation of the voters. The power of the executive has been weakened almost to impotence by mass opinions and pressures. This has led the democratic states to commit mistakes that could be fatal.[84]

---

[83] Lippmann, *Public Philosophy*, p. 50 n. 4.
[84] Ibid., pp. 51, 53–54.

The Public Philosophy was begun, so the author informs us, before the Second World War, but not published until 1955. What he says about the mistakes of the executives in the democratic states applied fairly accurately to France and Britain in the thirties, though not to the United States. From the vantage point of 1955 it would appear that in 1939 to 1941 the strong executives in the fascist and Nazi and some of the communist states made the disastrous miscalculations. But Lippmann is concerned with a longer period of time and is deeply fearful of the results of the loss of faith of the greater portion of democratic peoples in "intangible realities." His reasoning becomes especially difficult to follow when he goes on to say that since the First World War almost every Western government has had its difficulties, but the constitutional monarchies have proved more durable, more capable of maintaining both order and freedom, than the European republics.[85] It is not clear whether the comparative stability comes from a lesser degree of secularization or the presence of constitutional monarchs. Lippmann does not mention that in the comparatively stable countries there was a long tradition of constitutional self-government, an agreement upon fundamentals —including the relations of church and state.

Similarly, the chapter on the totalitarian counterrevolution (VI) is limited to discussion of the countries where antiliberal and antidemocratic movements and governments have upset constitutional democracies that had never been firmly or long established. Lippmann is wrong to suggest, on the basis of these examples, that taking governing power from the large electorate and giving it to an élite corps indicates the weakness, or decadence, of modern democracy. Similarly, it is a mistake to cite the failure of popular government where it had never succeeded or, as in the case of Russia and perhaps Germany before 1914, where it had never been given a period in which to find its way. It is bad history and poor analysis to give weak popular government as the

[85] Ibid., pp. 55–57.

cause of the failure of democracy in these countries, several of which (West Germany, perhaps Italy) have had more effective self-government since 1945 than ever before.

The brief chapter is, however, of relatively little importance to Lippmann's central argument, as appears in Chapter VII. Here we begin with another of those Götterdammerung statements: "We are living in a time of massive popular counterrevolution against liberal democracy."[86] Western liberal democracies have failed to ease the fears and suffering of this century. They have not been able to govern in an age of turbulence and war or to preserve the principles necessary to sustain a liberal society. The evil that entered and that has caused failure even in the most stable of great Western democracies (Britain and America, at this point) is Jacobinism—a form of anarchism, as contrasted with the spirit of the American Revolution and the Constitution. The Jacobin creed of the French Revolution entered England as Radicalism in the nineteenth century. It had an early American disciple in Tom Paine, but it did not gain popular acceptance until the time of Jackson. The Americans of the Revolutionary and Constitutional generations were not against government, but against misgovernment. The Jacobins, on the other hand, following Holbach and Rousseau, provided a new doctrine that promised salvation and rebirth. It was a Christian heresy. To replace the solitary struggle of each soul within itself, they offered a single, vast collective redemption. But the New Adam followed in the footsteps of the old. And still the fate of democracy has been ventured on belief in the Jacobin doctrine. That doctrine is the accepted theory in mass education, for it offers a solution to an apparently insoluble problem—that of educating quickly and adequately the rapidly growing masses who are drifting away from their social and political heritage.[87] The schools have to do far too much, or rather attempt too much. They must try to assume the duties of dying social institutions, to carry on the traditions of Western civilization. The Jacobin doctrine merely evades the problem of how to govern a mass

[86] Ibid., p. 63.
[87] Ibid., pp. 66–73.

society. Rousseau, Pestalozzi, and Froebel are the philosophers who held that the good faculties of man would unfold during life; only the bad ones were acquired. Little government is therefore needed and little training in the art of governing. Those disciplines concerned with faith or ethics can be eliminated from the curriculum. The most the schools (and colleges) are expected to do is prepare students for careers; there is no standard of learning and a public philosophy is omitted as useless to success.[88]

Marx and Engels, though scholarly and sophisticated men, were Jacobins to the extent of believing that one great class revolution could, after a period of proletarian dictatorship, end the age-old system of class struggles. It remained for Lenin and other communists of the next century to declare that the period of revolution would be continued indefinitely. Consequently Lenin, Hitler, and Stalin did not flinch from any means necessary to reach their goals. Why? Because "the inhuman means are justified by the superhuman end"; instruments of historical necessity, they have been "appointed to fulfill the destiny of creation."[89]

It is interesting to watch Hitler being slipped into this list. In some respects he belongs there, though not as an interpreter of Marx. He did give the impression of having a mission to save his country, if not the world; he was a powerful executive, but he also relied, in a way and to a degree not found in Russia, upon mass support, a mass driven to hysteria and frenzy by his demagogic appeals. And he operated not in a half-primitive, semiliterate, unindustrialized country (the Russia of 1917), but in one of the most advanced countries of the West so far as science, learning, rigid discipline in family and community, and industrialization were concerned. Only in the absence of a tradition of constitutional self-government were the Germans objectively different from the small democracies of the West or from Great Britain and the United States. They had also been defeated in the First War, a defeat they never fully accepted, any more than they accepted for long the harsh provisions of the Versailles Treaty, a treaty

[88] Ibid., pp. 73–78.
[89] Ibid., pp. 79–83.

that is neither one of the great achievements of peace-making nor the monstrously infamous document Hitler and his followers accused it of being.

At any rate, Lippmann sees Lenin, Hitler, and Stalin as totalitarian Jacobins of the twentieth century—men who rejected the older and softer doctrine and took upon themselves and a small élite the role of redeemers, viewing their assumption of godhood not as deadly sin but as triumphant human destiny. This involved the reversal of the traditions of civility; it meant a continuing "war with the human condition": it was contrary to the morality of "finite men" and was against freedom, justice, the laws, and order of the good society as they are expressed in the traditions of civility and in the public philosophy.

Having discoursed on the failure of the Western liberal democracies, largely because of weak and dependent executives, and of the totalitarian communist and Nazi regimes, which substituted overly strong executives with superhuman conceptions of their mission, Lippmann comes, in Book Two, to the public philosophy. He begins by defending the importance of ideas and principles in the creation and preservation of the good society. He ends the first brief part of this chapter with an exhortation to transmit the traditional wisdom of civil society to the citizens of the present and the future. Unhappily, even the democratic societies are rejecting the very traditions which gave birth to the finest form of their way of life. They no longer follow the principles of the public philosophy which are essential to the liberal democratic society. "In Toynbee's terrible phrase, they are proletarians who are 'in' but are not 'of' the society they dominate."[90]

What Lippmann means by the term, the *public philosophy*, a phrase that is far from self-defining, is somewhat clarified on the next page. It appears that in the seventeenth and eighteenth centuries men in the Western nations had worked out and adopted a system of limitations on the monopolies of church and state. These operated not only in religion, philosophy, and morals, but also

[90] Ibid., p. 96.

in science and learning. They were embodied in constitutions and bills of rights; they restricted the limits of sovereignty whether it was monarchial, parliamentary or congressional, or popular. This public philosophy was "the doctrine of natural law, which held that there was law 'above the ruler and the sovereign people ... above the whole community of mortals.' "[91] This public philosophy, or doctrine of a higher, natural law, was based upon many centuries of philosophy—from the Stoics and St. Thomas Aquinas to more modern times—and had been embodied in documents like Magna Carta, the Bill of Rights of 1689, the Declaration of Independence, and the first ten Amendments to the Constitution. The greater part of the public philosophy was never explicitly stated, but the tradition of civility did, in the West, furnish standards of conduct, both public and private, which nurtured and upheld freedom and democracy.[92] The men who established the institutions of democracy espoused the public philosophy. They had witnessed the corruption of power and so believed that governments should be limited, not given sovereign powers. The higher law remained a higher standard of law and administration.

It is not quite clear when the decline from the standard of the public philosophy, of civility (seemingly synonymous with public philosophy), of natural law, began. But the public philosophy, or civility, or natural law is the foundation of the institutions of Western society. Without this foundation, these institutions will fail.[93]

Following this sweeping generalization there is a brief historical survey of the development of the doctrine of a natural law that provided a standard by which the actions and legislation of men could be judged. This quick survey is based on excellent sources, ancient and medieval, but it of course has no reference to the

[91] Ibid., p. 97. The quotation is from Gierke's *Political Theories of the Middle Age,* an anachronistic source for ascertaining the doctrines that came to be accepted in the seventeenth and eighteenth centuries.

[92] Ibid., p. 99.

[93] Ibid., p. 101.

hideous injustices of slavery, peonage, serfdom, to the plight of
lowly agricultural workers who were only nominally free, or of
those who did not follow the official religious creed of the time
and place.

From about 1500 to 1800, the West experienced the rise of the
national modern state, the increasing division and specialization
of labor, and also, for this is not here mentioned, the Reformation
and Counterreformation, with the accompanying convulsions and
persecutions, of which the Thirty Years' War and the Inquisition
were only the most horrible. "The new school of natural law was
able to meet" the needs of those great changes "until the end of
the eighteenth century."[94]

In the nineteenth and twentieth centuries natural law came to
be looked on as outmoded, antidemocratic, even reactionary. The
ancestral order was left to those who could appeal to the "anomic
mass," Hitler among them. This mass was " 'anonymous, . . . without an authentic world, without provenance or roots,' " without,
that is to say, a creed to live by.[95]

In the relativistic morality of the present, "there is no public
criterion of the true and the false." We lack that public philosophy
which was the creation of Zeno and the Roman lawyers, which
was transmitted to the modern age through the doctrine of natural
law. The great question is whether the ideas of the public philosophy can be recovered and reestablished among enlightened
men.[96]

The first conception that must be accepted and used as a guide
is the law and the tradition of private property as a social institution. Nineteenth-century individualists did grave injustice to
the theory of private property because they understood a great
deal about the rights of private property and scarcely anything

[94] Ibid., pp. 104–108, 109.

[95] Ibid., pp. 109–112. Lippmann has been quoting Spengler, Hitler, Gide,
Durkheim, and Jaspers, authors who did not live in countries with a heritage
firmly grounded in the tradition he praises. His references to David Riesman's
Lonely Crowd and to Toynbee's proletarians are applicable to many stages of
Western civilization, not just to that of recent times.

[96] Ibid., pp. 114–115.

about the reciprocal duties. The choice as they saw it lay between Manchester and Marx. This is misleading, for the whole concept of private property is one of rights and duties under the law.[97]

The choice between Manchester and Marx was, of course, a false antithesis in the West, and indeed few accepted it as valid. The course of legislation in the industrially advanced countries indicates that beyond any question.[98] There was, in these countries, little desire to abolish private property but a growing tendency to regulate many aspects of it, especially as the forms became larger, more intricate, and more powerful.

Lippmann's brief discussion of the right of freedom of speech, of the right to disagree and to express that disagreement, is limited by the statement that that right is qualified, that the speech must have meaning, be free of foolishness or deceit. Under present circumstances often freedom of speech does not mean free discussion but rather degraded opinion.[99]

Freedom of dissent has been grossly misused by the opponents of democracy to establish regimes that then deny to their opponents the right to dissent. True enough in such countries as Italy, Germany, and in certain Latin American republics, where the element of mass violence, of force, even of coup d'état by a military junta has been all too frequent.

The real point would seem to be that there is no objective test of rationality in debate. It is easy to think of dozens of changes or reforms bitterly opposed by the defenders of the status quo as irrational, if not downright revolutionary. Most of the major developments in the system of political philosophy Lippmann wishes to reestablish were just that—to those who opposed them—from the time of King John, the Stuarts, George III, the defenders of the Articles of Confederation, to very recent times. Further, it is less self-evident than Lippmann believes that the established Western democracies came "apart" and into a state of "collective

[97] Ibid., pp. 121–122.
[98] See, for example, A. V. Dicey, *Lectures on the Relation between Law and Public Opinion* (London, 1905).
[99] Lippmann, *The Public Philosophy*, pp. 126–129.

amnesia" in the twentieth century. They have, to repeat, made grave and costly errors, but, compared with the suicidal mistakes of the old regimes in Russia and China or the weakness and instability of democracies of Italy and Spain, their record is one of remarkable consistency, though it doubtless lacks much of the wisdom of the kind of public philosophy yearned for by perfectionists, particularly by those having the advantage of 20-20 hindsight. The examples of Socrates, St. Thomas Aquinas, and Cardinal Newman are valid when one is writing about the "aristocratic code,"[100] but they have only a remote relation to the world of the mid–twentieth century. They represent lofty and moving examples of what is best in men, but governments have rarely been guided by such men, or, if they have, rarely with prolonged success in staving off disaster.

Diversity in the present world is inevitable, and so the great words—liberty, justice, equality, fraternity—have a variety of meanings, none applying to all circumstances. The ideal and the actual cannot be the same. Absolute rule by the church is as unacceptable as political absolutism. There must be a balance. It is essential that church and state be "separate, autonomous, and secure. But they must also meet on all the issues of good and evil."[101] Even this apparently temperate statement becomes clouded when one realizes that in our country there is not one church but scores of churches, none having a majority of the population, most being almost minuscule except in their own conviction of righteousness. As Lippmann says, there are so many variables that "governing is not engineering but an art." This leads him to fall back on the doctrine, as old as Aristotle, of the balance of power, not "as an instrument of aggression and defense," but "as the structural principle of public order in the good society."[102] That was also the theory of Madison, Jefferson, John Adams, of most of the founders.

The final chapter (XI) is "The Defense of Civility." The public

[100] Ibid., pp. 135, 140.
[101] Ibid., pp. 154, 155.
[102] Ibid., pp. 155, 159.

philosophy has taken many forms, but all have held to the principle of Cicero (and many others), that "law is the bond of civil
society." This was the premise of those who founded free institutions. Unhappily today's democratic societies have forsaken the
primary laws and teachings and the general mode of thought that
Lippmann has termed the public philosophy. Its future depends
upon whether the public philosophy can be received and applied.
The great question then is whether this old doctrine or set of
principles, formulated before the industrial revolution, can be re-
worked for the technological age. If this cannot be done the
liberal democracies face the totalitarian challenge without a public philosophy free men can believe in, for mere agnosticism,
neutrality, and indifference do not provide such a faith; those who
lack belief simply don't care very much.[103]

In the democracies of the present time the Jacobin ideology is
the popular doctrine. This ideology lacks the essentials of the
public philosophy—discipline, order, the rule of law. Materialism
has been substituted for the ideal of belief, which is "the realm of
immaterial entities." The problem of "communicating impondera-
ble truths to common sense" when these truths cannot be tested
against fact is and has always been immense. Yet it is essential
that "reason shall regulate the will, that truth shall prevail over
error."[104]

What is this truth? This reason? Its essence seems to be that
everyone is bound by contract in a constitutional system. Only
then is there freedom from tyranny, whether that of ungoverned
rulers or that of ungovernable crowds. Only under contract does
power have any legitimacy. The great contractual documents of
the Anglo-American tradition were of this kind, though they
could not cover the unwritten laws of society. The author suggests, citing Bentham, that many have abandoned belief in this
concept because actually "there never was an historic contract"—
a statement that would have been rejected by the men who wrote
and adopted the first American state constitutions. Those men

[103] Ibid., pp. 160–161.
[104] Ibid., pp. 162, 164, 165.

saw their work as formulating a contract that instituted a "civil body politic." This is another instance when Lippmann would have done well to have studied American constitutional history more thoroughly and to have relied less upon Gierke, Bentham, and Blackstone. Similarly, there is no doubt that most of the Americans of the eighteenth century accepted the idea of natural law. The question is rather which natural law we are to accept today, for the term has had many meanings in our own country; it is not, as Lippmann assumes, a single body of doctrine.[105]

The critical disciplines are those of philosophy and theology. Lippmann hopes, though he does not guarantee, that, if the teachers would return to the principles of the public philosophy, the decline of the West could be halted. Certainly if they continue to stand against its restoration decline cannot be halted. Most contemporary men are, in practice, opponents of constitutional democracy and consider the public philosophy discredited. What they favor is the Jacobin idea of the absolute sovereignty of the people. The decline of Western civilization has been brought about through the misrule of that sovereign.[106]

Lippmann sees contemporary society in the West as a condition of "anomie" (without law or order, especially natural law), descending into barbaric violence and tyranny. The defenders of civility are those who oppose this decline. They require and must have the "seals of legitimacy, of rightness and of truth." If we are to act effectively we must be convinced of the righteousness of the action. Once men have that conviction of righteousness, of conscience, they possess, according to Confucianism, "the mandate of heaven." "In the crisis within the Western society, there is at issue now the mandate of heaven."[107]

---

[105] Ibid., pp. 167–170; Benjamin F. Wright, *American Interpretations of Natural Law*, ch. XI.

[106] Lippmann, *Public Philosophy*, pp. 178–179.

[107] Ibid., pp. 180, 181.

6. From Scientific Realism to Romantic Renaissance

It is tempting to view Lippmann's nine "books of political philosophy" as steps in the transformation of a young and optimistic liberal into an old and pessimistic conservative. No one who reads the books consecutively can fail to see this major shift in his theory, though the books written during the short period in which he was enthusiastic about the New Deal (*The Method of Freedom* [1934] and *The New Imperative* [1935]) temporarily altered the otherwise almost perfect curve. But such a simplistic summary of what is the most interesting group of books on or about political theory written by an American in the twentieth century is inadequate. Obviously the hopeful exuberance of his youth, especially as set forth in *Drift and Mastery*, is far removed from the largely critical view of most changes in the world in *The Good Society* and even further from the deep gloom of *The Public Philosophy*.

One recent author has seen these writings as a "twentieth

century pilgrimage."[1] He apparently views Lippmann's many changes of doctrine and methods of reasoning as progress toward the light of religious faith, something he does not quite attain, since "at the present stage of his pilgrimage, Lippmann's underlying affirmation remains one of faith in man, rather than in God."[2] My own view is that his faith in man was badly shaken before 1922 and exceedingly pessimistic by 1955. On one point I agree with the author of *Twentieth Century Pilgrimage*. The central problem of Lippmann's political theory is his difficulties with that stubborn and ubiquitous problem of all political philosophy— what Lippmann's teacher Graham Wallas called Human Nature in Politics. Since the invention of political theory as we of the West understand and differ about it, from, that is, the time of the Greeks, the capacities and reactions of men as individuals, in groups, and in states have been the basic, though not always the acknowledged or explicitly discussed, foundation of every serious attempt to build a philosophy that will contribute to an understanding of organized society.

Most of the other themes, doctrines, or conclusions, including his proposals for forward change or for return to the glories of a former age, are in some way related to this central concept. But there are several others that deserve separate consideration. Among them are the role and capacity of government, the place and importance of laws, both human and natural, and of man-made constitutions, the function and the future of science, the sanctity of property, the uses of both history and prophecy, and Lippmann's relationship to the more than four decades in which he was writing.

[1] Charles Wellborn, *Twentieth Century Pilgrimage: Walter Lippmann and the Public Philosophy*. Dr. Wellborn, university chaplain and associate professor of religion at Florida State University, appears primarily concerned with Lippmann's "significant faith in the relevance of a moral universe and realm of absolutes" (p. 185), and the variations in his theory of politics are indicative of "Lippmann's unfolding pattern of insight into man's value which has been accompanied by an increasingly sophisticated understanding of human nature" (p. 148).

[2] Ibid., p. 185.

Perhaps I should say before discussing this variety of changes in assumptions and conclusions, changes I consider unequalled in the entire history of political theory, that I do not believe consistency is necessarily a virtue. A change of doctrine or of assumptions may be caused by changes of circumstances, social, economic, or political, by increased knowledge, of the past, of science or technology, or of other less easily classifiable kinds, or simply by maturity. Lippmann was a very young man when he wrote his first two books, and age, as well as many changes in economic and political conditions and problems, would almost necessarily have resulted in shifts in his theory of politics. Indeed, rigid consistency has often been indicative of both intellectual and provincial limitations, as well as stubborn adherence to what were believed to be the interests of a class or a section, or both, as with Fisher Ames and John Taylor of Caroline. Among Americans of the first rank there are very few, other than John Marshall, who never changed position. But with Lippmann there is not just the one change, from liberal-progressive to conservative-reactionary. There are so many of what Holmes might have called interstitial variations, modifications, and reversals that it is difficult, perhaps impossible, to find adherence to any discernible basis for formulating a philosophy of politics that deserves the respect and the standing easily accorded to numerous portions of the books.

Consider first the theories of human nature. Lippmann's study with Graham Wallas, as well as with James and Santayana, saved him from the naive and eternally sunny view of human nature in the mass that one finds in romantics like Tom Paine, perhaps Rousseau, or, to come closer to Lippmann's time, Eugene V. Debs, and any number of bleeding-heart reformers who argued that if only some particular change were made—the abolition of monarchy or of slavery, the change from capitalism to social or common ownership, a single tax on land, a tariff for revenue only, free coinage of silver, women's rights, the short ballot, the initiative and referendum—all would be well, corruption ended, good and wise men elevated above bossism or control by the interests. Even in his *Preface to Politics*, Lippmann, optimistic progressive though he was, opted for leaders who would lead, though his admiration for Theodore Roosevelt as the antithesis of a routineer in politics, seems less well founded today than it did in 1913. *Drift and Mastery* indicates an even greater faith in the collective ability to achieve what Herbert Croly had a few years earlier discussed in *The Promise of American Life*. Underlying this faith in the ability to change drift to mastery of economic, social, political, and technological problems and mistakes is an almost eighteenth-century concept of human rationality. The voice of the people may not be the voice of God, but, with the aid and guidance of wise leaders devoted to the public well-being, rational results will be attained.

Perhaps the view Lippmann inherited and, in spite of the warnings of Graham Wallas (who remained a Fabian socialist), exemplified in his early books was not far removed from the optimism of the men who wrote, adopted, and applied our first state and our national constitution. They were not wide-eyed innocents who believed that all men, or even a majority, were good, wise, and moved by rational processes in their political decisions. They did believe in what Hamilton, in the first paragraph of the *Federalist* essays, referred to as the possibility "of establishing a good government from reflection and choice" rather than depending forever on "accident and force." Without exaggerating the extent of their inheritance, it is probable that they were in some measure indebted to Locke's *tabula rasa* theory of reason, the idea that man starts with nothing except a blank slate upon which the external environment can inscribe an accurate picture or impression of itself. This view assumes an essential equality, so that all men have approximately the same ability to perceive society's problems and to arrive at a rational judgment about solutions. Even by 1787 Locke's philosophy had undergone modifications, and by 1913 it had been further transformed. Yet the prevailing doctrine of the progressive era, of which Lippmann is an exemplar, holds to a belief in general rationality and in the capacity to recognize the need for improvement, given leaders who themselves are not routineers, who see the light ahead and can show the way to the land of promise and social mastery.

If this is a fair summary of the conception of human nature in Lippmann's first two books, it is far from that in his two books on public opinion and, in important respects, more remote from his final position. Put bluntly, in *Public Opinion* and in *The Phantom Public* Lippmann—by quotations, citation of authorities, and reliance on his observations as a journalist—asserts the essential triviality and irrationality of human nature, its unreliability as a source of wise decisions in public affairs, and then calls on his fellow humans to behave as if they were concerned only with rational means and ends. He is unwilling to discard at least the general structure of liberal democracy, yet his devastating analysis of the defects of the nature of public opinion, following the opening quotations from Plato's majestic allegory of the cave and Hamilton's assertion in the privacy of the Convention that the voice of the people was not the voice of God, requires that conclusion. *Public Opinion* is an important book, though it would more clearly remain in the first rank of all books on the subject if the final Part VIII, "Organized Intelligence," and especially its final chapter, "The Appeal to Reason," were omitted. *The Phantom Public* adds nothing to the analysis and makes an even more impossible proposal for redressing the failures that result from the irrationality and general infirmities of human nature.

Perhaps *The Method of Freedom* in 1934 reflects a more optimistic view of the possibilities inherent in human nature, though it can more profitably be viewed under the next heading—the role and capacity of government. But surely the assumptions, if not explicit statements, of *The Method of Freedom* are not those of the books on public opinion, and they are hopelessly remote from Lippmann's position in *The Good Society*. For two years Lippmann apparently regained the sanguine attitude of his youth about the need for and even confidence in active and energetic leadership, in this case of the second Roosevelt. Only a few years earlier in *A Preface to Morals* he had seen government as a relatively inactive force, a mediator among rather than a leader of free people in bringing an end to the inequities and excesses of unrestrained economic enterprise. In *The Method* he substitutes a Keynesian theory of free collectivism. To be sure, the system of a "compensated economy" does not spring from the collective wisdom of the mass, but the attitude of the great bulk of the people is assumed to be far different from that depicted in the books on public opinion. The free collectivism depends upon strong executive leadership and also upon the capacity of the people to understand and follow the (elected) leaders. This is apparently impossible in states where there is both widespread ignorance and general economic insecurity, where the mass of people are indeed proletarians. Given a favorable economic base, something comparable to Aristotle's polity or Jefferson's ideal in a pre-industrial age, the populace will respond. Lippmann does not clearly or adequately, much less systematically, relate his temporarily hopeful view of human nature in politics to the action of the leaders. He suggests difficulties only to brush them aside, but it is an essential presupposition of this conception of a free and democratic society that the mass will be responsive in a regime of compensated economy.

Only three years after *The Method of Freedom* and two years after the essays in *The New Imperative*, Lippmann published his much longer and extraordinarily different *The Good Society*. In this book he despairs not only for the wisdom and capacity of the mass of men, but also for the leaders, in the democracies and in the totalitarian states, who believe organized control is compatible with liberty. Human affairs have become unmanageable. Power must be limited. All the great gains in liberty of the past thousand years have been on the limitations of rulers. Not more democracy, however, but less control is the aim. Collectivism, which in one form ("free collectivism") had been praised in *The Method of Freedom*, is here condemned because it is beyond the capacity of men to direct without establishing tyranny. Planning and an "administered society" are enemies of freedom in the Western democracies as in the communist, fascist, and Nazi states. Men seek their own interests, not only in a war economy but also in time of peace, and human nature is too selfishly defective to stand the strain of the resulting conflicts.

J. M. Keynes was apparently the mentor in *The Method of Freedom*. Adam Smith is certainly the guide in *The Good Society*. After but hardly below Adam Smith come the founders and interpreters of the common law. The free market rests upon a basis in law, as well as upon the removal of restrictions imposed by king or parliament, or dictator, or, apparently, president and Congress.

This book might, if only certain sections are read, be seen as a program for greater democracy for all men, since the continuing argument is against restraints on liberty. Nevertheless, there is no expressed or implied enthusiasm for rational and just behavior by the general run of men, except as men deal with their own individual affairs. Human faculties are limited and government must be geared to these limitations. It is not in the collective wisdom of the people, nor in that of legislative assemblies, that Lippmann places his trust, but in restraints on power, the true free economy of Adam Smith, the law of the courts, and the spirit of a higher and more universal law than any made by men.

In his final book of political theory, *The Public Philosophy*, begun in 1938 but not completed and published until 1955, Lippmann writes that he is a "liberal democrat." Yet he clearly and emphatically asserts that the liberal democracies have not only declined in influence and in power, but have lost their way; mass control has failed. Critically wrong decisions have been made by them. Human nature evidently had the opportunities as well as the power before 1917, but the result was "the decline of the West." There is no hope in more democracy or, if I read him correctly, in better protection of civil liberties. A stronger executive takes the place of the advance of popular government as understood in the nineteenth century or in the progressive era of his youth. One of the curiosities of the argument is the defense of stronger executives in the age of Stalin, to whose despotism he was bitterly opposed, not to mention Hitler, an executive who was as powerful as he was both wicked and, finally, fatally wrong in his decisions; and not many years after the energetic leadership of Franklin D. Roosevelt, whom, after the first two years of the New Deal, he believed to be leading the country away from the liberty of its traditions. Whatever the inconsistencies in the argument, it is clear that Lippmann despairs of human nature as a source of wisdom and decisions that promote what he now chooses to call "civility" and "the public philosophy." The masses, and their representatives, have lost contact with the traditions of Western society, and a return to those traditions is our only hope. This classic conception of a golden age in the past is variously located as before 1914, before 1870, and before 1789. Jacobinism, a surprising term to apply to the constitutional democracies of Western Europe and the United States, has usurped the place once accorded to natural law. At times it appears that natural law was that embodied in bills of rights and similar documents, but his emphasis is not on rights but on right, not on the expansion of liberties but on an order of civility, of tradition, and there is rarely any reference to the horrors of slavery, peonage, or serfdom, or of the fourteen-hour days in the mines and mills for men, women, and children all widely found in that age of civility when the public philosophy prevailed.

Lippmann's views of the role and capacity of government reach their high point in *Drift and Mastery*, decline in the books on public opinion, and are almost consigned to the shelf in *A Preface to Morals*. They rise again in *The Method of Freedom*, for the free collectivism and compensated economy necessarily require an active government that intervenes to stabilize the economy, even when its actions go contrary to the immediate will of the citizens. But in the later, and much more popular and widely read books, *The Good Society* and *The Public Philosophy*, the role of government appears to be more nearly negative than positive. The legislative branch is only a doubtful source of law, though there are some inconsistencies on this point in *The Good Society*, as there are in references to Maine and Spencer. Its decisions are less to be trusted than those of the courts or than, most especially, the inherited wisdom embodied in natural law and the traditions of civility.

It is useful, I think, to go back to the hopeful views of *Drift and Mastery* and place them beside those of the final books in the series to see how great is the change. In the book published in 1914 he asserts that "the profoundest change that has ever taken place in human history" is a "loyalty that looks forward," the substitution of "purpose for tradition." This requires that we choose our ends, then select means. There is, he finds, a far clearer vision of the future at that time than in the nineteenth century. The "bogeys" and superstitions that formerly held us back have been laid and, by collective, usually governmental, action we can attain a new freedom. Democracy is "a weapon in the hands of those who have the courage and the skill to wield it." Government action, including government ownership of much of industry, is assumed to be desirable, as well as possible.

Even in *Drift and Mastery* there is little enthusiasm for legislatures, despite the fact that legislation had been responsible for most of the great reforms, including the original Bill of Rights, and that only through legislation could most reforms be attained. Yet in this book there is less suspicion of representative legislatures than in any of the others here considered. To be sure, improvements are needed in the structure of government, and the bad sociology found in the court decisions of recent years must be altered or set aside, but government can be the primary factor in the first goal, that of lifting all men "above the misery line." The larger aim of democracy is "the richest life that men can devise for themselves." Democracy in politics "is the twin-brother of scientific thinking," and in 1914 Lippmann could give no higher ranking to the possibilities of positive action by concerted political action.

By 1937 collective action and science are alike demoted, feared, replaced by tradition, by economic and legal philosophies of the past, most typically of the eighteenth century. By 1955 the age of science, like the age of governments seeking to eradicate the worst of inherited evils—social and economic, as well as those more explicitly pertaining to religion, to sexual relations, to the taboos or bogeys of the past—are all repudiated, strongly condemned, or merely ignored. The hopeful attitude toward the achievements both of political democracy and of science are replaced by a longing for the restoration of what Lippmann, using the term he borrowed from Sir Ernest Barker, who found it in the writings of Coventry Patmore, somewhat hazily calls the "great traditions of civility."[3] Without repeating what was earlier pointed out about the wretched conditions in which the great mass of men lived in that age, it is allowable to suggest that here again Lippmann is doing little more than longing for something that is past, that he seeks to avoid the harsh realities of an age of science, technology, overpopulation, and ecological blunders, not by political action but by appeal to the splendid side of an age that is gone. Of course he asserts that what he calls "the public philosophy"—as though there were only one such creed and it pertinent to all our problems—is of great practical value. This can be attained, however, only if the public philosophy once again is accepted and adhered to. How this can be done in view of the decline of the West, in the face of the rising barbarity of the mid–twentieth century, he never makes clear, but I think he discarded both science and the democratic society, as he now saw it, as instruments. It is almost a call for a retreat to the cloisters, to the life of contemplation and of faith. Unless I have completely misinterpreted the last two of Lippmann's books on political theory, his conception of the roles of both government and science had turned full cycle between 1914 and 1955. Despair had succeeded hope.

This transformation of attitude and of conclusion is almost as striking when one turns to the place of law and constitutions. Legalism, law, and lawyers were anathema to Lippmann in 1913.

---

[3] Walter Lippmann, *The Public Philosophy*, p. 3, n. 1. Though Lippmann uses the word repeatedly, he never indicates how much more weight it is to carry, or what meanings it has, beyond the dictionary definitions—typically: good mannered, courteous, or (usually labeled "archaic") civilization, culture, good breeding.

It was a tremendous mistake to turn our government over to lawyers, "who deal in the most verbal and unreal of all human attainments." He is happy that the "vital part of the population" has
pretty well emerged from any dumb acquiescence in constitutions
and applauds the first Roosevelt for helping to cast down this idol
(though, in 1937, he was bitterly opposed to the second Roosevelt's court reform, or court-packing, bill). It is the mechanical
limitations of constitutions to which he objects. It should be
remembered that in 1913 the courts, particularly the federal
courts, following the lead of the Supreme Court, had not begun to
expand the meaning, or even very often to apply the most limited
and literal reading, of the provisions of the Constitution guaranteeing various civil liberties. Nevertheless, Lippmann's argument
is not for an expansion of these guarantees of rights, but for a
politics unshackled by the laws and constitutions of the past or by
the verbalisms of lawyers and judges.

By 1937 the Good Society is to be based on the free economy of
Adam Smith and his true followers (who usually do not include
Herbert Spencer or the Social Darwinians) and upon the foundation and the protection of the common law. Coke and Blackstone,
even the authors of the American Constitution, have become the
heroes and models, where earlier they had been barriers to progress. This transformation is completed in *The Public Philosophy*
when natural law is revived as the true faith.

That natural law had a very long history and an exceedingly
important role in the development of political theory is too obvious to require comment. That it did not have a single form or
content is equally evident to anyone who reads that history. Even
when the subject is limited to American usage, there are at least
eight meanings of *natural* or *nature* in the seventeenth to the
twentieth centuries, and the content of natural law and natural
rights varies from extreme radical to ultraconservative.[4] It is far
from clear which natural law Lippmann is appealing to, or which
meanings he attaches to natural law, except that he means a reviv-

[4] Benjamin F. Wright, *American Interpretations of Natural Law*, ch. XI.

al of a concept that belongs somewhere in the past—possibly, though this is not certain, in the age before the development and use of the natural rights doctrine as part of natural law, a development rarely found before the Protestant Reformation with its emphasis on the right of each person to decide his religion and, to a varying extent, his destiny. The concept he ranks so highly is not a meager or an unknown one; it simply belongs to a former age.[5] Most of us would agree that a greater respect for what Lippmann presumably means by *civility* would be desirable in the present state of society (more so in 1973 than in 1955), but an appeal to natural law as a force to bring that about seems futile, almost a cry of despair that we are not what our ancestors were—which is true enough in many ways, not all for the worse.

The variations in assumptions and conclusions are, as I have been listing them, numerous and substantial. None is more striking than that involving private property, very much including large-scale economic enterprise. In the first two books, especially *Drift and Mastery*, the author casually takes it as unnecessary of supporting logic that the rights of property are subject to appropriation and collective ownership and control. The time is sure to come when the government will operate basic industries, finance government enterprise out of the profits, eliminate interest, and substitute collective saving. Since there is no doubt that we can collectively finance such enterprises, the only standard is whether the appropriation of such economic enterprises can be carried on effectively and in the public interest, that is, whether it can contribute to the welfare of consumer and labor, eliminate waste, and generally change our "sooty life" into "something worthy of our dignity."

This sounds like socialism to most persons, but to the young Lippmann the American Socialist party had no appeal, nor did he appear to be bothered by the extent to which his proposals were

---

[5] A comparison of the variety of interpretations, meanings, and usages in, for example, seventeenth-century England, with those of the Medieval Church Fathers or the great Roman lawyers will make evident the vast range of meaning given to this fundamental concept of law and politics.

at odds with the prevailing system of economic life. He can, and does, dismiss the case in support of landlords or the capitalists as if his case for socialization of a large, though not precisely de-limited, area of traditional economic life represented no more than minor reform.

In *The Method of Freedom* he argues for governmental inter-vention to bring about a compensatory economy that will bring an end to the economic cycle of boom and crisis. The old laissez faire has to give way to a form of collectivism. Apparently this does not mean social ownership; certainly it does mean a very large meas-ure of social control of private property. He is careful to distin-guish between military collectivism, as under communism (and, as he was writing, under the Nazi regime in Germany), and free collectivism, especially that found in the English-speaking coun-tries and, he might have added, advocated by Keynes and those economists who saw the problems of economic life much as he did. The essence, then, of this free collectivism is to preserve the liberty of private transactions, evidently including the continua-tion of great and basic enterprises, and restoration of balance, when needed, by public action as directed by a popularly selected government. Intervention in economic affairs is both allowable and essential, not to achieve state socialism, in the sense of public ownership, but rather to redress grievances, to protect the weak against the strong, even to prevent the strong "from accumulating excessive wealth and power." The right to work is a natural right and, as such, to be guaranteed and protected.

Three years later, in *The Good Society*, protection of the weak against the strong through government intervention had become something out of the remote past, a past that jumps from feudal lords to absolute monarchs to the pharaohs. About the only quali-fication he had in his opposition to the attempts of the New Deal to regulate the power of property was an opposition to monopoly, though the eradication of monopoly, if that is what he intended, was to be achieved by following the true doctrine of Adam Smith —the principle of the freemarket and the distribution of labor. How the views of the greatest of English economists, who published *The Wealth of Nations* in 1776, when the industrial revolution was barely getting underway in his own country and the technological revolution of a century and more later was not dreamed of, could be applied in 1937 is not told. Rhetoric again takes the place of explicit explanation, even the explanation of applicable principles. At any rate, corporate enterprise is praised; corporate collectivism (which could easily mean varieties of monopoly or quasi-monopoly) is "a thousandfold" less dangerous than state collectivism. The youthful vision of public ownership of basic industries has given way to a dread of government ownership, of even the relatively mild forms of government regulation in New Deal legislation, much of which was application on a national scale of what various cities and states had been doing for at least a generation, often for a century.

I find it impossible to see the change from *The Method of Freedom* and *The New Imperative* to *The Good Society* (a book of 401 pages that could not have been written, even by the facile Lippmann, in a few weeks) as one following any known rational process of economics or political theory. Few persons reading the history of those years would conclude that all the measures of the New Deal were wise, or consistent with each other, or, just as important, successful in bringing an end to a depression of unprecedented proportions. But there was nothing between 1935 and 1937 that could account for the startling change from warm praise to an indictment equating the American legislation with the return to the "heresies of absolutism . . . the choice of Satan." Lippmann's praise of the centuries in which there had been the increasing emancipation of individuals from old tyrannies of feudalism, of church and state, is certainly valid, though he ignores the general acceptance in the colonies of the countries of western Europe, including England, of slavery, an institution outlawed centuries before in England and in western Europe. Most of us would agree that the absolute rule of Stalin in Russia and Hitler and his followers in Germany were new and harsh forms of absolutism, but the legislation of the United States Congress was not comparable in kind or manner of enforcement.

The policies of the second Roosevelt were logical applications of what the first Roosevelt, Lippmann's political inventor in 1913, had accepted—assumption of national responsibility for what had become a national disaster. The national legislation of 1933–1937 was probably more defective in not going far enough in its attempts to deal with appalling problems of hunger and unemployment, to protect rights of individuals in economic and social as well as political fields, than in its alleged drive toward the revival of a new tyranny. It is a wry commentary upon the New Deal measures, most of which have long since been taken for granted and absorbed by all major parties, that, though many of them brought some measure of relief, it was not until after the nation began to rearm and to sell billions of dollars of supplies and munitions to the allies attacked by Germany that the country, including the great corporations, returned to full employment and general prosperity.

It remains a mystery how Lippmann in 1937 could see a close similarity, virtually an identity, between the Russian Planning Commission and the use of public money for public works in the United States. Not only has Lippmann reversed his own doctrines; he has abandoned the very possibility of securing economic stability—including feeding the starving and securing employment for millions of jobless—by collective action. A planned and administered society for the United States is now treachery to freedom, a system that will lead only to the multiplication of pressure groups seeking special benefits and special privileges. Just how the extension of Adam Smith's free market and division of labor will end the economic depression, which in 1937 had lasted for nearly eight years (longer in some parts of the economy), is not spelled out. Lippmann glorifies the productivity of free trade and the freedom of economic enterprise without facing the fact of the economic cycle of boom and bust. He does not oppose all reforms; some he believes necessary. But the basic system remains one that does not interfere with the free market, the division of labor, the interdependence of mankind, and the absence of collectivism. Collective control should come primarily from a common law, though not the mistaken and reactionary decisions of the United States Supreme Court in the four decades before 1937. Just how the courts could assume this burden is left vague. In spite of his criticism of the Supreme Court's due process and, he should have added, some of its commerce clause and tax decisions, he, like Hamilton in the seventy-eighth *Federalist*, placed a degree of trust in the wisdom of the judiciary that he thought misplaced when given to elected representatives and that he had condemned in *A Preface to Politics*.

The whole of this extraordinary, widely read, and much-admired book is not only a reversal of views expressed in 1914 and again in modified form in 1934 and 1935; it is an essay in nostalgia, not for the days of his youth so much as for some imagined time in the seventeenth or eighteenth or nineteenth century, a time when there was undoubtedly tremendous economic growth and a wide variety of truly liberating movements, but also a time of economic and social inhumanity. Despair of the wisdom of the mass of men, which characterizes the two books on public opinion, is here transferred to those elected to govern. The size and complexity of economic life in the new age made collective control impossible if freedom was to prevail. General legislation to control this vast complexity is found in absolutist states, and there takes the form of militarized despotism.

So far as concerns the rights and limitations on private property and the failure of governmental or collective planning, *The Public Philosophy* of 1955 adds little to *The Good Society* of 1937. Presumably, though this is not explicitly set forth, the general acceptance of much of the collective legislation of the 1930's by the Western constitutional democracies was one of the reasons for the lamented decline of the West. Just how the strengthening of the executive (or the selection of executives who are wise, just, and strong) or the revival of natural law would repeal either the economic cycle or lead to lower taxes and greater liberties for all is not delineated, though the distrust of elected representatives is clearly evident. Nor can one discover precisely what the relation is between a renewal of the tradition of civility and the end of poverty and discrimination.

Doubtless the leaders of the Glorious Revolution of 1688 (nobility, gentry, upper middle class in the cities and towns) reflected an aura of civility, as they were responsible for the great Bill of Rights in 1689. But the existing system of property remained unchanged. It will be remembered that Locke used the word *property* so broadly that it included life, liberty, and estates. For the majority of Englishmen, in cities and especially in the country, their condition was, and remained until well into the nineteenth century, not far removed from serfdom. Conditions in the early factories—and this was substantially true for over half a century after Adam Smith wrote—were miserable by any standard acceptable in this century or by any allowable meaning of civility. But to Lippmann, in this final attempt to state a philosophy for what he believed to be the anomie of the 1950's, the need was not for greater social justice, or civil liberties, or the eradication of the greatest evils of acute poverty; it was for a revival of Cicero's conception of law as the bond of society, for a return to a conception of civility located somewhere in the remote past.

In most of his books here dealt with, especially in the last two, Lippmann appeals frequently to history to support his arguments. Yet his history is selective, and not always reliable, sometimes clearly inaccurate. It is substantially correct that he never developed a sound sense of history or a background of historical learning adequate to support his broad generalizations. Nor is he consistent in his history, particularly when dealing with the history of the American colonies or the very great last quarter of the eighteenth century of his own country. The men who framed our original state and federal constitutions, at first, mechanical in their thinking and planning, were later the great innovators of modern constitutional democracy. His knowledge of the man Tocqueville called the "most powerful advocate democracy ever had" is so slight that Jefferson is made the model for the anti–New Deal, right-wing Liberty Leaguers of 1936.

Perhaps what bothers me most is Lippmann's air of assurance when he is reversing his field, as he often did, or when he relies upon antithesis (planning *or* free society, anomie *or* a return to natural law of the eighteenth century or of the Roman lawyers, rationality *or* irrationality) when what is needed is the making of distinctions. Thus in the books on public opinion he produces a theory of the omnicompetent citizen as a necessity in a successful liberal democracy. The men who founded and developed the theory of representative democracy had no such illusion. They recognized the defects Lippmann describes and sometimes exaggerates, but they also believed that it offered the best possibilities for the future, if based on written constitutions incorporating what Madison called "auxiliary precautions," a system of multiple deliberations with which both John Adams and Jefferson completely agreed. And any realistic student of liberal democracy (Lippmann to the last so classifies himself) recognizes that it is not great wisdom so much as information concerning the needs and desires of the public that is possible, or most nearly possible, in such a system. He had himself so written in *A Preface to Politics*, but that very important idea was abandoned by the time of *Public Opinion*. Surely the return to natural law or to the self-adjusting free market bolstered by the common law of Coke and Blackstone would not bring that about.

Among the most interesting aspects of Lippmann's nine books of political theory or public philosophy is their relation to the time in which they were written. *A Preface to Politics* and *Drift and Mastery* are among the best reflections of the optimism and the faith in progress of the Progressive era. They are tracts for the times. Some parts of the Progressive platform of 1912 were too democratic for him, but he caught and exemplified the spirit of the liberalism of the years before the First World War.

The two books on public opinion reflect the disillusion widely held by many journalists, novelists, and dramatists in the years following that war. Varied, yet not inconsistent expressions are to be found in the writings of H. L. Mencken, and in the first years of his *American Mercury*, in the novels of Sinclair Lewis, John

Dos Passos, Scott Fitzgerald and others of the "lost generation," in plays of O'Neill, in writings from Paris, New York, the Midwest, and the Deep South.

Even *A Preface to Morals* reflects a point of view toward politics characteristic of many in the age of Coolidge and Mellon. And *The Method of Freedom* is clearly an expression of the euphoria of the first year or two of the New Deal. Lippmann does not even question the overly ambitious and ill-fated catchall (a partial imitation of the corporative state), the National Industrial Recovery Act, a measure declared unconstitutional by the Supreme Court in 1935, two years before *The Good Society* appeared.

In the seven books published between 1913 and 1935 Lippmann shifted his position four times, but he was, in important respects, in harmony with major tendencies in the United States. He was, that is to say, in harmony with his environment.

It is with *The Good Society* that Lippmann begins to express a view of society radically at variance with that of his time and place. Unlike the reformers or the revolutionaries of left or right, he does not propose reforms or basic changes in society, economics, and government so much as a return to the ideology and the systems of the eighteenth or even the seventeenth century, to the age of Adam Smith, bolstered not by the new Supreme Court, but by Blackstone, Coke, and, finally, Cicero. There are, to be sure, passing suggestions that he longs for the liberalism of the years before the First World War, but the nature and thrust of his argument would not take in or applaud the Republican administrations of the 1890's or what Lincoln Steffens called "the shame of the cities," or what Bryce had earlier labeled the county governments: the "dark continent" of American politics. It is a fair assumption that he would not in 1937 have praised the miserable working conditions in a large proportion of American factories and mines, or the racial discrimination then generally taken for granted. On these subjects, however, he is generally silent, at least after *Drift and Mastery*. He says nothing in 1937 (or 1955) about the political corruption of the Grant or Harding administrations, or the lackluster presidency of Coolidge, or the robber barons, the conspicuous and vulgar display of wealth, or the grinding poverty of millions in cities and on farms.

With *The Public Philosophy* Lippmann seems to have lost contact with the times in which he lived and wrote and in which his syndicated column was one of the leading, possibly the foremost, editorial commentary. His yearning for civility is easy to sympathize with.[6] A greater measure of civility (no matter how defined) is a fine, though a very limited, ideal. The question is, how do we attain it? Surely not by the return to one of the conceptions of natural law of the Stoics, the Roman lawyers, or the seventeenth or eighteenth centuries. The argument is that our constitutional system was founded on the premises of natural law. This is not much more relevant to the issues and problems of the mid-twentieth century than the more accurate statement that it was made for a people living in an age of what Beveridge in his *Life of John Marshall* called "community isolation," when some ninety percent of the population was rural. The members of the Convention of 1787 did take many assumptions from the political philosophy of the preceding century and a half, but any reader of Madison's record of the debates in that Convention will find that their immediate sources were a combination of experience, observation, and personal knowledge of the limitations of the Articles of Confederation, and of the experiments of the states with their new constitutions, as well as recollections of colonial politics. Perhaps foremost was a general acceptance of a theory of human behavior in organized society as they knew it, which is best expressed in the ratification controversy in *The Federalist*.

As James Madison was the principal, though certainly not the only, author of the Constitution, it is not beside the central point to remark that he used what was both a broad and an intensive

---

[6] It is interesting to speculate on the reason why Lippmann chose the word *civility* instead of such possibilities as *humanity*, *dignity*, even *liberty*, or such traditional phrases as *equal justice under law*. There is no difficulty in understanding why he did not select *democracy* or any of its synonyms. Is it incorrect or unfair to him to say that in making this choice of words he was demonstrating a long-standing, though not always expressed, longing for aristocracy?

knowledge of the history of government, especially of federal governments, in both the debates in the Convention and his remarkable essays in *The Federalist*. Compared with the scholarly Madison, Lippmann, in his appeals to history and natural law, is an inconsistent and unreliable amateur. More important is the contrast between Madison's focus on solving the immediate problems confronting the weak and sorely divided country in 1787–1788 and Lippmann's longing for what he believes to be the civility we have lost, presumably because we have ceased to rely on the precepts of natural law—though, to repeat, he never defines civility except where he makes the curious statement that it is natural law or tells us which of the many doctrines of natural law we should revive and cling to. Madison and his fellows of the first great age of constitution-making were building for the future, employing all the learning and the experience they had, not longing for the past. Lippmann, in a less troubled age (for the West was certainly stronger and even less divided than were the colonies and states in 1776–1788), despairs of the time of his maturity and sees in the seventeenth and eighteenth centuries amenities and principles he had scorned in his earlier books.

The more one considers *The Good Society* and *The Public Philosophy*, the stronger becomes the conviction that Lippmann had come to be out of joint with his time. He could not face the very real difficulties of his own stage in history and attempt to propose a philosophy of politics that might aid in bringing about a method or a principle for dealing with them. Consequently he wrote, in these two appealing and interesting books, something only a little less like a dream world set of proposals than Edward Bellamy's immensely popular *Looking Backward*, that literary fantasy of 1888. Bellamy set out to write a novel set in the year 2000 and ended with a charming romantic utopia. Lippmann set out to deal with the eternally tough and never completely resolved problems of society and politics and ended with a vision of an idealized past—and a hopeless present. It remains a mystery how an exceptionally able journalist, continuously dealing with the affairs of "Today and Tomorrow," as his syndicated column was headed, could have concluded his final statement of political philosophy, or public philosophy, by a rejection of such achievements as there were in his own times and have substituted a plea for a renaissance, a revival of the golden, though presumably not the sordid, features of an age that has past.

It would be possible to make two collections of statements found in these nine books. The first would consist of sentences, sometimes short paragraphs, remarkable for their perceptiveness, their value for the understanding of politics and society, their accuracy of prophecy, even their exceptional wisdom. The second collection would consist of statements that are just as clearly incorrect, or farfetched, or inappropriate, almost preposterous, whether relating to history or to contemporary institutions and needs. Fortunately the first anthology would be much, much larger than the second, but, when one sets out to analyze and assess the political theory of this man who wrote more books on politics that have been very widely read and usually highly praised than any other man of his long career, the second cannot be ignored. They give a human dimension to a man who usually wrote as though he spoke from Olympus, if not from Sinai.

Whether there has in fact been a decline of the West is by no means certain. There has, of course, been a tremendous decline in colonialism, especially in Africa and India. There has also been a very great expansion of communism, so that it extends, though not in a monolithic bloc, from East Berlin to the Pacific. It is equally true that the Nazi and fascist destruction of civility and constitutional democracy in western Europe ended in 1945, and that there now appears to be no serious threat of their reemergence. Lippmann's gloomy "Decline of the West" in 1955 is the more curious when we recall the extent of the Nazi conquest in 1941 and the end of that power in 1945. The Nazi conquest of Europe is comparable to that of Napoleon in the early years of the nineteenth century, but it was more barbarous and left fewer, if any, positive achievements.

The rise of communism—the real threat in 1955 and today—is not comparable to the overthrow of ancient civilization by the barbarian hordes and the coming of the dark ages, from which modern civilization emerged, or began to emerge, a thousand years later. Perhaps a closer parallel is the spectacular success of the Moslem conquests after the prophet Mohammed brought the word to a small, nomadic, previously uninfluential group of Arabs. Within a century that tribe had become a vast force that swept across northern Africa, occupied Spain, threatened France, was defeated at Tours, spread through most of the Balkans, and moved eastward to the Pacific. At the present time, twelve hundred years later, it is, though not so formidable as it was five hundred years ago, one of the most powerful and unsettling forces in the world—as witness the civil war in India when it became independent, and the persistent conflict between Israel and its neighbors in the Middle East.

There is no way of knowing whether the great victories of communism in Russia, China, and the satellite countries of Europe will, centuries from now, continue to threaten the economic, social, and political states of the West. It now seems, despite Lippmann's obituary, that the West is not only alive but flourishing. Natural law is not the major instrument of political thought that it was in the age of the Stoics, the Roman lawyers, Aquinas, the sixteenth to eighteenth centuries, nor does it seem likely to be revived, though that is always a possibility. If it were revived, under that or another name, we cannot know how it would be interpreted or on which side it would be used. It could not have the particular meaning that it was given two or three hundred years ago.

It has been remarked that Lippmann, in the books published in 1937 and 1955, appears to have little interest in supporting the rights and the needs of the poor, the disadvantaged by reason of color or environment. The expansion of minority rights doctrines by the Supreme Court that began in 1925 and was steadily supported by the Hughes Court is not referred to.

Civility, to repeat, is a good, though limited, virtue in society.

We could well do with more of it now, and this generalization applies to many countries, including those behind the Iron Curtain. Probably the need is greater today than in 1955. The causes are many and there is no agreement about all of them. In the United States the migration of hundreds of thousands, probably millions, of people from backward agricultural (and cultural-educational) areas to the cities is one of them, a movement resulting from more than one cause, though change in agricultural technology is certainly a major factor.

Another major cause of the decline in what Lippmann apparently means by civility is the increasing dissatisfaction with and opposition to the long continued war in Vietnam. This too cannot be attributed to mass demand or the dominance of Congress. This decision or, rather, multiple decisions are made by the executives and their official, expert advisers. Strong executives can be as harmful to civility, to the society Lippmann longs for, as mass actions, and the history of the twentieth century since 1917 would appear to support the very opposite of Lippmann's plea for executive leadership. This is as true in Nazi-communist countries, not to mention scores of military dictatorships in South America and Africa, as in the United States. Indeed, it is in the East rather than in the West that there has been a great decline in civility, in traditional values expressed by natural law, in western standards of liberty and justice. The East, from East Berlin to the China Sea, has gained in power and centralization of authority, not in the standards Lippmann apparently has in mind. Only Japan appears today to be nearer to his ideal than before 1941, and that came only after a terrible war, defeat, military occupation, and possibly an excessive imitation of western industrial technology.

One final observation about Lippmann's place as a writer of political theory. It is no more allowable to relegate him to the dust bin of those who have written insignificant books on the theory of politics because his proposals in the books on public opinion and the two published in 1937 and 1955 do not solve the problems he raises than it would be to say that Plato and Rousseau are insignificant because *The Republic* and *The Social Contract* do not provide practicable solutions to the questions they raise and discuss. The point is rather that he repeatedly shifts his focus as well as his proposals for solution. There seems to be no essential unity of conviction as to aims, in addition to a bewildering variety of means, each offered with an air of conviction. If his analysis of problems is nearly always timely and pertinent, his proposals for solution become less relevant to their time. They are not, however, frivolous, and they have not only become widely read but have received their full share of praise. He may be the "most important political thinker" of this century, though this statement is, unintentionally, a commentary on the quality of political thought in twentieth-century America. He has not gone in for what many believe to be the obscurantism of a great deal of the sociology and the political science of his later years, but neither has he made use of substantial insights and conclusions made by scholars in the same period.

It is unlikely that future scholars will find Lippmann's books of political philosophy of the stature of books by, say, Locke or Rousseau. Nor is it probable that any of the books will have the durability of *The Federalist* or the writings of Jefferson, though it is always possible that one or more of his books will attain that rank.

As I stated earlier, I find Lippmann the most interesting political theorist of his time, though I do not argue that he is the most influential. My interest is engaged not by the number of his books of political theory but by the number of problems or issues he discusses, by the variety of his approaches to the problems of a liberal democracy in the twentieth century, and by the changes in method and in conclusions. He has read widely, though often hastily and sometimes superficially, in the literature of history, economics, and political and legal philosophy. It is not meant to be condescending to remark that his books of political theory are in a different classification from those of other journalists. He has set himself higher goals and is therefore to be compared, in these books, as distinguished from his columns and many of his essays, with major figures in the history of American political theory. Considered in that way, it seems doubtful that he will attain the position that he has sought. The unprecedented variety of conclusions, which makes him interesting, does not compensate for his failure to face the difficulties of his time. And while his writing is always clear, usually forceful, often "dignified and stately," it lacks the quality to arouse emotional sympathy, nor are there sentences that remain in one's memory, as in the finest writings of Jefferson or Lincoln or Holmes or, for that matter, Tom Paine. The rhetorical flourishes with which he ends several of the books are, unhappily, not worthy of the importance of his subjects or of the many passages with which each of the books is enlivened and enriched.

BIBLIOGRAPHY

BOOKS BY WALTER LIPPMANN

Drift and Mastery. New York: Mitchell Kennerley, 1914. Paperback edition by Spectrum, 1961.
Essays in the Public Philosophy. Boston: Little, Brown and Co., 1955. Paperback edition by Mentor Books, The New American Library, 1956.
The Good Society. Boston: Little, Brown and Co., 1943. Paperback edition by Grosset and Dunlap (n.d.).
The Method of Freedom. New York: Macmillan, 1934.
The New Imperative. New York: Macmillan, 1935.
The Phantom Public. New York: Harcourt, Brace and Co., 1925.
A Preface to Morals. New York: Macmillan, 1929. Paperback edition by Beacon Press, 1960.
A Preface to Politics. New York: Mitchell Kennerley, 1913.
Public Opinion. New York: Harcourt, Brace and Co., 1922. Paperback edition by same publisher, 1960.

OTHER BOOKS

Beard, Charles A. *Economic Interpretation of the Constitution.* New York: Macmillan, 1913.
Bellamy, Edward. *Looking Backward.* Boston: Ticknor and Co., 1888.
Brown, Robert E. *Middle Class Democracy in Massachusetts, 1691–1780.* Ithaca: Cornell University Press, 1955.
Bryce, James. *The American Commonwealth.* New York: Macmillan, 1888.
Childs, Marquis, and Reston, James, eds. *Walter Lippmann and His Times.* New York: Harcourt, Brace and Co., 1959.

Croly, Herbert. *The Promise of American Life*. New York: Macmillan, 1909.

Dicey, A. V. *Lectures on the Relation between Law and Public Opinion in the Nineteenth Century*. London: Macmillan, 1905.

Hamilton, Alexander; Madison, James; and Jay, John. *The Federalist*. Edited by Benjamin F. Wright. Cambridge: Harvard University Press, 1961.

Harrod, R. F. *Life of John Maynard Keynes*. London: Macmillan, 1951.

Hartz, Louis. *The Liberal Tradition in America*. New York: Harcourt, Brace and Co., 1955.

Holmes-Pollock Letters. Edited by Mark Howe. 2 vols. Cambridge: Harvard University Press, 1931.

Holmes, Oliver Wendell. *Collected Legal Papers*. New York: Harcourt, Brace and Co., 1931.

Kenyon, Cecelia M. *The Antifederalists*. Indianapolis and New York: Bobbs-Merrill, 1966.

Klein, L. R. *The Keynsian Revolution*. New York: Macmillan, 1947.

McCloskey, Robert G. *American Conservatism in the Age of Enterprise*. Cambridge: Harvard University Press, 1951.

Mill, John Stuart. *Representative Government*. Edited by A. D. Lindsay. New York: E. P. Dutton, 1950.

Roosevelt, Theodore. *Letters*. Edited by Elting E. Morison and John M. Blum. 8 vols. Cambridge: Harvard University Press, 1951–1954.

Rossiter, Clinton. *Conservatism in America*. New York: Alfred A. Knopf, 1955. Paperback edition by Vintage Books, 1962.

Rossiter, Clinton, and Lare, James, eds. *The Essential Lippmann*. New York: Random House, 1963.

Schlesinger, Arthur, Jr. *The Crisis of the Old Order*. Boston: Houghton Mifflin, 1957.

————. *The Coming of the New Deal*. Boston: Houghton Mifflin, 1958.

Sinclair, Upton. *The Brass Check*. Pasadena: Privately printed, 1919.

Steffens, Lincoln. *Autobiography*. New York: Harcourt, Brace and Co., 1931.

Tocqueville, Alexis de. *Democracy in America*. Edited by Phillips Bradley. New York: Alfred A. Knopf, 1945.

Wallas, Graham. *Human Nature in Politics*. London and New York: Macmillan, 1908.

Weingast, David Elliott. *Walter Lippmann: A Study in Personal Journalism*. New Brunswick, N.J.: Rutgers University Press, 1955.

Wellborn, Charles. *Twentieth Century Pilgrimage: Walter Lippmann and the Public Philosophy*. Baton Rouge: Louisiana State University Press, 1969.

Wright, Benjamin F. *American Interpretations of Natural Law.* Cambridge: Harvard University Press, 1931.

———. *Consensus and Continuity 1776–1787.* Boston: Boston University Press. Paperback edition by Norton, 1967.

———. *The Growth of American Constitutional Law.* Boston: Houghton Mifflin, 1942. Paperback edition by Chicago University Press, 1967.

INDEX

absolute collectivism: definition of, 76; and capitalism, 77

absolutism: importance of, 33, dependence on, 35; uniform principle of, 114; acceptability of, 130; forms of, 146

Adams, John: on human nature, 23; and patronage, 50; and the national Constitution, 60; on the balance of power, 130; mentioned, 48, 150

Agricultural Adjustment Act: constitutionality of, 89

Alexander the Great: 62

Alien Act: 50, 104

American Individualism: 84

American Revolution: and natural law, 112

Ames, Fisher: and government based on the will of the people, 54; mentioned, 135

anarchism: in New York in 1914, 27; and private property, 106; Jacobinism as form of, 124

Antifederalists: and separation of power, 50

Aquinas, St. Thomas: appeals to natural law by, 111; public philosophy of, 130; and natural law, 155

Aristotle: political theory of, 49; and public will, 62; on government by the middle class, 81, 100; on the balance of power, 130; mentioned, 138

Arnold, Benedict: 93

Articles of Confederation: executive power under, 104; limitations of, 152; mentioned, 129

authoritarianism: results of, 90–91; rise of, 94; method of governing by, 107

Babbitt, Irving: 33

Barker, Sir Ernest: on civility, 142

Beard, Charles A.: on the founders of the United States, 50; and planned society, 93

Bellamy, Edward: and utopias, 56; mentioned, 153

Bentham, Jeremy: and laissez faire, 77; liberalism of, 99; criticism of natural law by, 112; on the common interest of society, 120; on civility, 131; mentioned, 132

Bill of Rights, English: and natural law, 112; and universal suffrage, 120; as public philosophy, 127; and private property, 149

Bill of Rights, United States: as limitation on government, 103; and natural law, 112; as public philosophy, 127; legislative responsibility for, 141

Blackstone, Sir William: 132, 143, 150, 151

Brandeis, Louis D.: opinion of business of, 29, 39

Brass Check: 53

Broun, Heywood: 12

Bryan, William Jennings: Lippmann's opinion of, 20, 30

Bryce, James: 45 n., 49

bureaucracy: effect of war on, 107; regulation of power of, 109

Burke, Edmund: conception of community of, 120; mentioned, 73

Cade, Jack: opinion of lawyers of, 20

capitalism: preservation of, 28; and political power, 67; governance of industry under, 68; effect of World War I on, 73; exceptions to free competition in, 74; and absolute collectivism, 77; failure of, 83–84

Chafee, Zechariah: and freedom of speech, 52

Chase, Stuart: 92, 114

Childs, Marquis: 9

Cicero: on civility, 131; conception of law of, 149; mentioned, 151

civil liberties: value of, 52; danger of loss of, 86

Civilian Conservation Corps: and the right to work, 82

Civilian Works Administration: and the right to work, 82

civility: decline of, 127; Lippmann's defense of, 130–132; traditions of, 142; importance of, 155–156. SEE ALSO public philosophy

Civil War, United States: reasons for, 95; mentioned, 116

Coke, Sir Edward: 112, 143, 150, 151

collectivism: emergence of, 74, 92, 93; kinds of, 75; and compensated economy, 77; failure of, 91, 115; as force of disunity, 94–95; conflict of, with liberalism, 96–97; as result of progressivism, 105; conflict of, with private property, 106; in *Method of Freedom*, 138, 145

common will: emergence of, 47

communism: as result of desire for security, 74; as expression of public opinion, 77; rise of, 155

compensated economy: necessity for, 76, 77–78; as means for economic stability, 78; and guarantee of right to work, 82; as source of security, 87; failure of, 91; theory of, in *Method of Freedom*, 138, 145

constitutionalism: mechanical aspects of, 21; Lippmann's writings on, 22

constitutional monarchies: effect of World War I on, 123

Coolidge, Calvin: social doctrine of, 73; mentioned, 65, 119, 151

corporate collectivism: dangers of, 89

Croly, Herbert: progressivism of, 11; on reform, 17; opinion of business of, 30; and collectivism, 136; mentioned, 26

Debs, Eugene V.: Marxism of, 32; on human nature, 135; mentioned, 13, 17

Declaration of Independence: as public philosophy, 127

democracy: Lippmann's attitude toward, 28, 58; image of, 49; theory of, 51, 56; failure of, 54–55, 118, 126; role of public opinion in theory of, 58; proposals for reform of, 59; belief in, 104; softness of, 117; problems of, 122; Jacobinism in, 125, 131, 140

Democracy in America: 48

determinism: nature of belief in, 32; in socialist theory, 47

de Tocqueville, Alexis: on democracy in America, 48; on Jefferson, 149; mentioned, 49

Dickens, Charles: social criticism by, 117

division of labor: revolutionary nature of, 96; mentioned, 145

Dos Passos, John: 150–151

Drift and Mastery: point-of-view of, 26; summary of, 26–37; political theory in, 38; optimism in, 39; view of human nature in, 136;

view of role of government in, 140, 141; view of private property in, 144; relationship of, to time when written, 150; mentioned, 133

due process: and the Supreme Court, 106, 148

economists: importance of point of view of, 44

elections: as expression of popular will, 60

Eliot, T. S.: 12

Engels, Friedrich: social criticism by, 117; as Jacobin, 125; mentioned, 12

environment: man's relationship to, 41–42

Essays in the Public Philosophy: summary of, 115–132; view of human nature in, 139; view of role of government in, 140; concept of civility in, 142; view of natural law in, 143; relationship of, to time when written, 152; mentioned, 29, 133

Essential Lippmann, The: assessment of Lippmann in, 9; organization of, 10–11; on *Method of Freedom*, 72

evolution: nature of belief in, 32

executive branch: power of, 119, 121; strength of, 148, 156

expertise: limitations imposed by, 44

faction: causes of, 46

fascism: as result of desire for security, 74; as expression of public opinion, 77

Federalist, The: Lippmann's understanding of, 18; rationalism in, 23; essays on causes of faction in, 46; and collectivism, 94; and popular opinion, 118; on protection of executive, 122; on government, 136; on the judiciary, 148; ratification controversy in, 152; mentioned, 157

Federalist party: 50

feudalism: as expression of public opinion, 77

Fitzgerald, F. Scott: 151

Fletcher vs. Peck: 103

Fourteen Points: 47–48

France: distribution of property in, 81

Franklin, Benjamin: 48

free collectivism: definition of, 76; and the right to work, 82

freedom of speech: Lippmann's attitude toward, 129

French Revolution: destruction of certitude by, 33

Froebel, Friedrich: on government, 125

General Theory of Employment, Interest and Money: influence of, on Lippmann, 91

Germany: constitutional democracy in, 79; distribution of property in, 81; social insurance in, 82; failure of freedom in, 115; mentioned, 35

Gierke, Otto von: 132

Good Society, The: view of New Deal in, 71; attitude toward Franklin D. Roosevelt in, 85; summary of, 87–115; condemnation of legislative control in, 110; view of human nature in, 137, 138; view of role of government in, 140; view of private property in, 145, 146, 148; relationship of, to time when written, 151; mentioned, 29, 115, 133

government: political structure of, 31; nature of, 68–69; and economic security of citizens, 74; and public opinion, 79, 118; function of, 83; limitations of, 90, 103; influence of pressure groups on, 92; role of judiciary in, 108; decline of, 119; problems of, 124–125; Lippmann's view of role of, 140–143

Great Britain: constitutional democracy in, 63, 69; social insurance in, 82; movement of, toward collectivism, 93

Great Depression: 11, 66, 68

Greeley, Horace: 10

guild socialism: 51

Hamilton, Alexander: and public opinion, 50; and patronage, 51; and government based on the will of the people, 54; and representative government, 58; and popular will, 60; financial policies of, 79; on protection of the executive, 122; on government, 136; on the judiciary, 148; mentioned, 48, 137

Hanna, Mark: 73

Harding, Warren G.: 119

Harvard Socialist Club: 24

Harvard University: Lippmann's attendance at, 12

Haywood, William D.: Lippmann's opinion of, 36

Hegel, Georg W. F.: and idea of man, 114

Hitler, Adolph: defeat of, 92; as collectivist, 95; and regimentation, 114; as Jacobin, 125; and natural law, 128; and executive power, 139; absolutism of, 146; mentioned, 57, 68, 82, 88, 103

Hobbes, Thomas: 11

Holbach, Paul d': as forerunner of Jacobins, 124

Holmes, Oliver Wendell: opinion of Roosevelt of, 21; speech by, on Chief Justice Marshall, 40; and due process, 103; mentioned, 135, 158

Hoover, Herbert: and Great Depression, 66; and collective action, 74; and the New Deal, 84, 89; abandonment of laissez faire by, 85

Hughes, Charles Evans: and the Republican Party, 47; and the Supreme Court, 107

humanism: as religion, 66

human nature: as basis for political decisions, 22; importance of, in politics, 25; Lippmann's theories of, 135–140

Human Nature in Politics: influence of, on Lippmann, 12, 39; revolt against rationalism in, 22–23; mentioned, 19

human will: Lippmann's conception of, 67

Hume. David: and division of labor, 98; criticism of natural law by, 112

idealism: materialism as substitute for, 131

individual freedom: Lippmann's view of, 89

industrial revolution: and liberalism, 98

industry: governance of, under capitalist system, 68

Italy: constitutional democracy in, 79; destruction of property in, 81; failure of freedom in, 115

Jackson, Andrew: and patronage, 50; mentioned, 63

Jacobinism: danger of, in democracies, 124; presence of, in democracies, 131; and sovereignty of the people, 132; application of, to democracy, 140; mentioned, 108

James, William: Lippmann's studies under, 12; on human nature, 135; mentioned, 46

Japan: seizure of Manchuria by, 88; mentioned, 35

Jefferson, Thomas: rationalism of, 48; political theory of, 49; and patronage, 50; on importance of public debate on issues, 62; and slavery, 79; on government by the middle class, 81; and democracy, 104, 149; on separation of powers, 122; on balance of powers, 130; mentioned, 63, 138, 150, 157, 158

Jones, Robert Edmond: 12

journalism: Lippmann's view of, 22

judicial branch: as problem solver, 30–31; function of, 105–106; enforcement of natural rights by, 106; protection of citizens by, 109

Judiciary Act of 1801: 50

Keynes, John Maynard: influence of, on Lippmann, 78, 138, 139; influence of, on Method of Freedom, 91, 145

King, Martin Luther, Jr.: 39

labor unions: importance of, 31; stereotypes in, 46

laissez faire: death of, 74, 87; and compensated economy, 77; impossibility of, 82; abandonment of, by Hoover, 85; Lippmann's denunciation of, 85; debate over, 97; and reactionary thought, 105; relationship of, to liberalism, 112–113; view of, in *Method of Freedom*, 145

Landon, Alfred: Lippmann's support of, 71

Lare, James: 9

lawyers: Lippmann's attitude toward, 20, 142–143

League of Nations: failure of, 88

Le Bon, Joseph: on common will, 47

legalism: tendency toward, 19

legislative branch: regulation of markets by, 109; condemnation of control by, 110; Lippmann's attitude toward, 141

Lenin, Nikolai: on social behavior, 47; and division of labor, 96; and regimentation, 114; on revolution, 125

liberalism: nature of absolutes in, 33; conflict of, with collectivism, 96–97; and industrial revolution, 98; philosophy of, 99; conception of government in, 107–108; relationship of, to laissez faire, 112–113; effect of World War I on, 150

liberty: Lippmann's definition of, 72–73

Liberty League: 149

Life of John Marshall: 152

Lincoln, Abraham: 63, 158

Lippmann, Walter: importance of, as political thinker, 9, 68; analysis of political philosophy by, 10; progressivism of, 11, 26; biography of, 12–14; interest of, in philosophy, 12, 18; affiliation of, with *New York Herald Tribune*, 13; affiliation of, with *New York World*, 13; work of, for Lincoln Steffans, 13; optimism of, 17, 26, 39, 136; statesmen admired by, 18; opinion of founding fathers of, 19; attitude of, toward science, 36, 141–142; as political theorist, 38, 133, 134, 156–158; influence of

Graham Wallas on, 39; and mysticism, 47, 114; opinion of moralists of, 67; attitude of, toward New Deal, 71, 133, 145, 149; distrust of pressure groups by, 80; attitude of, toward private property, 81, 144–149; denunciation of laissez faire by, 85; attitude of, toward individual freedom, 89; attitude of, toward monopolies, 89; interpretation of history by, 105; attitude of, toward executive power, 119; attitude of, toward public opinion polls, 121; view of Hitler, Lenin, and Stalin by, 126; definition of public philosophy by, 126–127; attitude of, toward freedom of speech, 129; defense of civility by, 130–132; theories of human nature of, 135–140; view of role of government of, 140–143; attitude of, toward legislatures, 141; appeals of, to history, 149–150; as voice of times, 153

Lochner vs. *New York*: 103

Locke, John: 112, 136, 157

Looking Backward: 153

Lunn, George R.: Lippmann's service as secretary to, 13

Machiavelli: 57, 69

Madison, James: on human nature, 23; on causes of faction, 46; rationalism of, 58; and the national constitution, 60; and collectivism, 94; and democracy, 104; and popular opinion, 118; on protection of the executive, 122; on balance of power, 130; knowledge of history of government of, 152–153; mentioned, 48, 63, 103, 150

Magna Carta: 127

Maine, Sir Henry: and progressivism, 117; on popular government, 121; mentioned, 140

Malthus, Thomas: and distribution of wealth, 98

Manchuria: seizure of, by Japan, 88

Man Versus the State, The: 92

Marshall, John: Holmes's opinion of, 40; and limitations on national government, 103; mentioned, 48, 135

Marx, Karl: and human motivation, 41; on social behavior, 47; and division of labor, 96; and idea of man, 114; social criticism by, 117; as Jacobin, 125; mentioned, 12, 32, 73

Mason, George: and national constitution, 60

Massachusetts Body of Liberties of 1641: view of lawyers in, 20; mentioned, 112

materialism: as substitute for idealism, 131

Mellon, Andrew: social doctrine of, 73; mentioned, 151

Method of Freedom, The: summary of, 71–83; as source of Lippmann's political theory, 72; optimism in, 75; models of compensated economies in, 86; comparison of, to *Good Society*, 89; influence of John Maynard Keynes on, 91, 145; attitude toward New Deal in, 133; view of human nature in, 137; theory of collectivism in, 138; view of role of government in, 140; view of private property in, 145, 146; relationship of, to time when written, 151; mentioned, 87

Mill, John Stuart: political theory of, 55; and importance of public debate on issues, 62; and laissez faire, 74, 77; socialism of, 76; and collectivism, 91

Milton, John: and freedom of speech, 52; mentioned, 112

monopolies: Lippmann's views on, 89

Montesquieu, Charles: principles of, 73; mentioned, 11, 18

moral codes: influence of, on public opinion, 45

More, Paul Elmer: 33

Morris, Gouverneur: 48

Morris, Robert: 48

Morris, William: and natural liberty, 67

muckrakers: usefulness of, 28

Mumford, Lewis: 92

Mussolini, Benito: defeat of, 92; as collectivist, 94–95

mysticism: Lippmann's opinion of, 47, 114

National Industrial Recovery Act: as extension of Hoover policies, 84–85; constitutionality of, 89; mentioned, 151

nationalism: as force for European unity, 94

natural law: examples of, 112; development of doctrine of, 127; decline of, 128; view of, in *Essays in the Public Philosophy*, 143; revival of, 148; as basis for United States Constitution, 153; as instrument of political thought, 155

natural rights: laws supporting, 101–102; importance of, in government, 106; historical instances of, 111–112

negativism: of liberal thought, 99

New Deal: Lippmann's attitude toward, 11, 71, 133, 140, 145; and Herbert Hoover, 84, 89; comparison of, to Russian Planning Commission, 147; mentioned, 74, 146, 151

New Imperative, The: summary of, 83–86; comparison of, to *Good Society*, 89; attitude toward New Deal in, 133; view of private property in, 146; mentioned, 72, 87

Newman, Cardinal: public philosophy of, 130

New Republic, The: founding of, 13

news: nature of, 53

newspapers: influence of, on public opinion, 52–54

Newton, Sir Isaac: 18

New York Herald Tribune: Lippmann's affiliation with, 13

New York World: Lippmann's affiliation with, 13

Nietzche, Friedrich W.: 26

Notes on Virginia: on separation of powers, 122

O'Neill, Eugene: 151

optimism: of Lippmann, 17, 39, 136

Paine, Thomas: and public opinion, 50; political theory of, 59; as founder of constitutional democracy, 63; as Jacobin, 124; on human nature, 135; mentioned, 158

Panama Canal: construction of, 29

Pareto, Vilfredo: criticism of natural law by, 112

Patmore, Coventry: on civility, 142

patronage: influence of, 50–51

Peel, Sir Robert: on common will, 47

Pericles: 90

Pestalozzi, Johann H.: on government, 125

Phantom Public, The: summary of, 58–64; view of human nature in, 137

philosophy: as critical discipline, 132

Plato: Lippmann's use of allegory of, 40; on poetry, 43; political theory of, 49; and utopias, 56; and perfect society, 57, 69; on statesmanship, 70; and the public interest, 121; mentioned, 20, 26, 31, 58, 61, 113, 137, 156

Political Economy: 76

political philosophy: analysis of, by Lippmann, 10

political psychology: Lippmann's use of, 20

politics: human nature in, 25; corruption in, 28; relationship of, to science, 35

Pollock, Sir Frederick: 21

popular will: elections as expressions of, 60; and progressivism, 104

pragmatism: possibility of, 35

Preface to Morals, A: summary of, 65–70; political theory in, 69; view of human nature in, 137–138; view of role of government in, 140; relationship of, to time when written, 151

Preface to Politics, A: philosophy presented in, 17; summary of, 17–25; view of democracy in, 38; conception of role of government in, 75; view of human nature in, 135–136; view of private property in, 148; appeals to history in, 150; relationship of, to time when written, 150; mentioned, 72

pressure groups: Lippmann's distrust of, 80; influence of, 91, 93–94

private property: definition of, 81; rights and limits on, 102, 148–149; and anarchism, 106; as social institution, 128; Lippmann's attitude toward, 144–149

productivity: decrease in, 29

Progressive Democracy: opinion of Theodore Roosevelt on, 26

Progressive party: 1910 platform of, 26; strength of, 30

progressivism: of Lippmann, 11, 26; and security, 101; dependence of, on popular will, 104; Lippmann's view of, 105; in Essays in the Public Philosophy, 117

Promise of American Life: opinion of reform in, 17; mentioned, 136

protectionism: rise of, 91

Public Opinion: as expression of change in Lippmann's political theory, 38; summary of, 39–58; view of human nature in, 137; appeals to history in, 150; mentioned, 22

public opinion: role of, in self-governing society, 43; influence of moral codes on, 45; constituents of, 47; role of, in theory of democracy, 58; influence of, 60; as creative force, 61–62; limitations of classical theory of, 63; traditional assumptions about, 76; and government, 118; importance of, 120; Lippmann's view of, 121

public philosophy: definition of, 126–127; application of, 131. SEE ALSO civility

Public Philosophy, The. SEE Essays in the Public Philosophy

Randolph, John: and government based on the will of the people, 54

rationalism: Lippmann's evaluation of, 19; reactions against, 22

realism: Lippmann's attitude toward, 25; in Drift and Mastery, 26

Reed, Jack: 12

Representative Government: 55

Republic, The: allegory in, 39; and the public interest, 121; mentioned, 58, 157

Republican party: disruption of, 30; as compact minority, 80

Reston, James: 9

Ricardo, David: and distribution of wealth, 98

right to work: as natural right of man, 82

Road to Freedom, The: attack on Franklin D. Roosevelt's programs in, 85

Roman lawyers: appeals to natural law by, 111, 152, 155; public philosophy of, 128

Roosevelt, Franklin D.: Lippmann's opinion of, 72; social doctrine of, 73; and Hoover, 74, 85; executive leadership of, 80, 140; mentioned, 89, 90

Roosevelt, Theodore: progressivism of, 11; third-party effort of, 17; attitude of Lippmann toward, 20; Lippmann's opinion of, 21, 136; and reform, 25; opinion of *Drift and Mastery* of, 26–27; opinion of business of, 29, 30; and mass action, 48; mentioned, 13, 28, 39

Rossiter, Clinton: 9

Rousseau, Jean Jacques: political theory of, 59; as nonfounder of constitutional democracy, 63; and the public interest, 121; as forerunner of Jacobins, 124; on government, 125; on human nature, 135; mentioned, 108, 156–157

Ruskin, John: and natural liberty, 67

Russian Planning Commission: comparison of, to New Deal, 147; mentioned, 92

Santayana, George: Lippmann's studies under, 12; on human nature, 135

Scandinavia: constitutional democracy in, 79; social insurance in, 82; distribution of property in, 81

Schlesinger, Arthur, Jr: 71

science: relationship of, to politics, 35; Lippmann's attitude toward, 36, 141–142

Securities and Exchange Act: as extension of Hoover's policies, 84–85

security: human motivation for, 74; compensated economy as source of, 87; and progressivism, 101

Sedition Act: 50, 104

Selden, John: 112

short ballot: Lippmann's attitude toward, 32, 135

Sinclair, Upton: on impartiality of the press, 53

single tax: Lippmann's attitude toward, 32, 135

Smith, Adam: and laissez faire, 74; influence of, on Lippmann, 91, 139; and revolutionary nature of division of labor, 96, 98; liberalism of, 97, 99, 106; and the Great Depression, 147; mentioned, 114, 141, 143, 149

Smith, J. Allen: on founders of the United States, 50

Smith, Sir Thomas: 112

Social Contract, The: and the public interest, 121; mentioned, 157

social Darwinism: and compensated economy, 77; and William Graham Sumner, 89; mentioned, 143

socialism: efficacy of, 29; and political power, 67; and compensated economy, 77; mentioned, 85

Socialist Club: Lippmann's activity in, 12

Socialist party: electoral activities of, 17; Lippmann's opinion of, 19; success of, 30

Social Politics Club: founding of, 12

social reform: methods of obtaining, 101

social science: state of study of, 57

Social Statics: 103

Socrates: public philosophy of, 130; mentioned, 25

Soule, George: 92

Soviet Union: revolution in, 68; distribution of property in, 81; absolutism in, 92; failure of freedom in, 115; and World War II, 116

Spencer, Herbert: and state influence, 92; liberalism of, 97, 101; and due process, 103; and human liberty, 108; and progressivism, 117; mentioned, 140, 143
Spengler, Oswald: 73
Spinoza, Baruch: and human will, 67
Spirit of the Laws, The: 73
stability: factors affecting, 100
Stalin, Joseph: as collectivist, 94; and regimentation, 114; as Jacobin, 125; Lippmann's opinion of, 139; absolutism of, 146; mentioned, 51, 88, 92
Steffens, Lincoln: Lippmann's work for, 13; mentioned, 151
stereotypes: role of, in formation of public opinion, 43–44; detection of, 46
Stoics: and natural law, 153, 155
Sumner, William Graham: and social Darwinism, 89
Supreme Court: Lippmann's view of, 30; as source of rule of law, 87; and due process, 99, 106, 148; role of, in government, 108; interpretation of the Constitution by, 143; and the National Industrial Recovery Act, 151; and expansion of minority rights, 155
Switzerland: constitutional democracy in, 79
Sydney, Algernon: 112

Taft, William Howard: Lippmann's opinion of, 20
Tammany Hall: 80
Taylor, John: 135
Tennessee Valley Authority: as extension of Hoover's policies, 85
theology: as critical discipline, 132
Thirty Years' War: reasons for, 95
"Today and Tomorrow": 10, 153
totalitarian counterrevolution: 123
totalitarianism: view of, in *The Good Society*, 88; natural rights under, 110
trade unions: 32
traditionalism: faults of, 36
Twentieth Century Pilgrimage: 134

unemployment: and anarchism, 27
United States: democracy in, 27, 63, 79; quality of life in, 34; collectivism in, 93
United States Constitution: Lippmann's attitude toward, 18, 32; grand conception of, 102; adoption of, 120; civil liberties guaranteed in, 143; basis of, in natural law, 152
utilitarianism: pleasure-pain psychology of, 41; rationalism of, 48; mentioned, 19

Versailles Treaty: 57, 118, 125

Wallas, Graham: Lippmann's studies under, 12; and rationalism, 22; opinion of *Preface to Politics* of, 25; influence of, on Lippmann, 39, 135; on human nature in politics, 134; socialism of, 136; mentioned, 19, 26
war: reasons for existence of, 95; effect of, on bureaucracy, 107
Washington, George: and patronage, 50
Watterson, Henry: 10
Wealth of Nations, The: influence of, on Lippmann, 146; mentioned, 97
White, William Allen: 10
Wilson, James: 48
Wilson, Woodrow: Lippmann's opinion of, 20, 30; presidential victory of, 30; social doctrine of, 73
women's suffrage: Lippmann's attitude toward, 32, 33–34, 135
World War I: Lippmann's government service during, 13; effect of, on progressivism, 26; use of symbols in, 48; effect of, on capitalism, 73; reasons for, 95; effect of, on government, 123; effect of, on liberalism, 150; mentioned, 57, 141
World War II: reasons for, 95; mentioned, 116, 118

Zeno: public philosophy of, 128